Janet M

D1448232

THE SPINNER'S WORKSHOP

a social history and practical guide

The Spinner's Workshop

John Mercer

Prism Press

Published in 1978 by

PRISM PRESS
Stable Court,
Chalmington,
Dorchester,
Dorset DT2 OHB.

Copyright 1978 John Mercer

Drawings by Susan Searight

ISBN 0 904727 77 7

Printed by A. Wheaton & Co., Ltd., Exeter

'Oh what a blissful place! By Severn's Banks so fair
Happy the Inhabitants; and Wholesome is thy Air . . .
New Bank, New Church, New Halls of great renown
New houses, new Flannel, new Gas in brave Newtown . . .
Go on and flourish, thy Markets ever bless
With Flannel, full, of Money and Success.'

(From a poem, 1833, on Newtown in Wales,
centre of the developing flannel industry

CONTENTS

ILLUSTRATIONS

Cover Woman spinning, 6th century BC, Sopron, Hungary
(incised on a pot of the Hallstatt culture)

Figures

CHAPTER 1

SPINNING AND ALTERNATIVE SOCIETY

If hand-spinning could be defined without much controversy, it is equally certain that 'alternative society' will raise different images for craftsman and industrialist, ecologist and scientist, socialist and capitalist, communitarian and citizen. Here the phrase refers to the dissenting, minority culture which at present exists within western society. Chadwick has recently summarised its scattered participation in and contribution to fields ranging from religion and politics through psychology, education and law to music, writing and the visual arts; equally important have been the experiments in co-operative work and in communal ownership and living. He writes that majority society has had 'the effect of permitting or actively cultivating aspirations towards a free, imaginative and creative life while in fact being incapable of fulfilling this promise.' This has led to the alternative minority culture, the product of educated, intelligent people, young rather than old, their aim to live in a more satisfactory society.

The culture has its other side, of course. Much of the movement uses its energies in fruitless protest against the old rather than in constructive work towards the new. For many it is simply an escape. Some choose to lose themselves in drugs and music. Others enter an undemanding world of astrology and unapplied Zen, of hobbits and rabbits, of self-oriented politics and hypochondriac psychology, whilst the means to life, such as their own food and health, become the real ends; forecasting general disaster, they fuss quietly about the comparative protein-content of different types of bean. Many go as far as collecting milk-bottle tops, in contrast to those who, less numerous, are intent on saving mankind by violent attacks on one or another aspect of society.

However, for a proportion of those who, deliberately or inadvertently, leave straight society, the aim is to work towards a more satisfactory *general* society. As Allaby has put it: 'In the years preceding the collapse of Roman civilisation there were those who had seized on a new idea that would provide the base for the civilisation that was to follow. The early Christians were reviled and mocked and feared for they threatened to undermine established ideologies. Today, again, the same groups of 'cranks', 'drop-outs,' 'weirdies,' 'hippies,' are reviled, and mocked, and feared, because they seem to reject established values.' In passing, it can be noted that, for some, the comparatively-uncomplicated belief in a personal responsibility to society has now replaced religion.

For many, whether serving a god or a society, personal responsibility now begins — as it has of course always done for the religious — with a scrutiny of the individual's own way of life. In 1976, the first European Sarvodaya Conference, towards a Gandhian, non-violent society, was held in London: the speakers emphasized that change would not just come from thinking in *sarvodaya* terms but required a material re-orientation in each person's life. Repeating 'love thy neighbour' was not seen as an effective antidote to a personal consumer pattern, for example, which involves exploitation and consequent aggressive feelings in a society elsewhere. Another example: to balance the mental and physical ill-health caused by his unsatisfactory work, industrial man turns to hobbies or to holidays for relief. And in many other ways western society both refuses to work at the causes of its malaises and tries to neutralise or escape from the multiplying symptoms.

Amongst the many proposals made at the *sarvodaya* conference, one came from the patriarch of the French community of L'Arche. Making twiddling motions with one hand and tugging at his rough tunic with the other, Lanza del Vasto told the meeting: 'You take a little stick and some wool . . . and you make a yarn . . . you take two sticks and you have a loom, on which you make your coat . . . . .'

The orientation of this book is towards the small contribution which hand-spinning can make in bringing about Chadwick's 'free, imaginative and creative life.' If the book proves useful to a few people then its aim will have been achieved. Only a mahatma or a lunatic aims to transform society — the realist hopes to multiply a little the good things which have been transmitted to him, inevitably either benefitting only a few or alternatively making an intolerable aspect of society a shade more tolerable.

Before coming to the craft itself, it will be necessary, then, to sketch out the personal and social losses to man which have resulted from the accelerating industrialisation of the last few centuries; this industrialisation is the basic cause of the alienation of those forming the dissenting culture. Alternative means of production will then be looked at briefly. Finally, some comments will be made on the craftsman in the small modern community. It hardly needs to be said that similar books can be written around every occupation producing man's basic needs of food, clothing and housing.

Industrial society and the individual

There is an element of choice in each individual's degree of participation in industrialisation. 'Modern wives so generally give way to luxury and idleness that they do not deign to carry the burden of manufacturing wool, and disdain clothing made at home,' complained the Roman Columella, adding that women were 'by a perverse desire pleased with clothing bought with a year's income.' In fact, far-sighted

Romans like Augustus were already deliberately wearing home-made clothes. It is no new thing to measure one's 'standard of living' by purchasing power and consumption — industrial man has sprung from dragons' teeth sown long before Rome. Schumacher has recently said that it is 'greed which delivered us into the power of the machine.'

'In these days of monster factories and steam machinery, whereby labour is concentrated and specialised, the tendency is to reduce the worker to the level of a mere machine, to obliterate his individuality, and so to do away with the purchaser's interest in the article, which does not show any special feature in its mode or manufacture,' words in fact written almost a century ago, by Ross as he recorded the crafts of the disappearing communities of the Scottish Highlands. Amongst the few attempts within modern industry made to reverse this dehumanisation of the individual have been those of the Work Research Institute in Oslo. Its head, Einar Thorsrud, has described the endemic diseases of industrial society: centralisation of command with increased bureaucracy, labour movement with disintegration of local communities, the separation of control from skill, specialist power, the substitution of electronic devices for human judgement and communication, the proliferation of rules and reports, the egocentric chasing of status. To these may be added the three-cornered struggle between work, money and leisure. The Norwegians are attempting to replace cash and status incentives by satisfaction arising from participation as a multi-skill worker in autonomous but co-operating groups which also have a share in overall management.

However, whilst such experiments are being made here and there — the English firm of Scott Bader embodies another — palaeo-industrialisation continues to spread across the globe. In 1976 the chairman of Massey-Ferguson Holdings explained that 'the difficulty of obtaining and keeping rural labour in many parts of the world has led to increasing interest in mechanizing farm production . . . the trend towards mechanized systems may not commend itself to some theorists in the West, but it derives,' he went on, somewhat simplifyingly, 'from a fairly widespread rejection of the exhortation: 'In the sweat of thy face shalt thou eat bread.' When, earlier in its evolution, industry was utterly dependent upon human robots, its psychologists produced the theory that man is an animal whose primary functions are to work and to consume . . . of course, the kind of work and the degree of consumption were not discussed. Now, with industrialisation continuing its disruption of more and more of the world's rural communities, the disoriented agricultural workers themselves are held responsible for the increasing spread of machines into farming: in fact it is simply the vicious circle resulting from both perennial capital's and modern labour's fixations on high cash rewards. The spread of industry across agricultural society follows the same pattern as did the struggle between industry and the craftsmen, now played out in all but a last few corners of the world, as will be seen from the next two chapters.

Conclusions reached only painfully and after a long circular process by 'civilised' society may seem obvious to a 'primitive' people. The Zulus say that unless there is harmony between an individual, his work and nature, disaster results. Schumacher has said that 'modern man has built a system of production that ravishes nature.' As for industrial man's work, it is uncreative, repetitive, lacking in room for initiative, with no sense of belonging; his superficially-opposed 'leisure' is also under the control of industry, so that his total way of life is imposed upon him — rather than being a harmonious development of himself and an individual note in his community. This western-origin sacrifice of man on the shrines of massive production and of profit contrasts painfully with the interpretation of 'right livelihood' by eastern thought such as Buddhism: work should be a common task which both produces the essentials of life and develops those taking part.

Alternatives to industrialisation

Parallel to the humanising experiments *within* industry there have been schemes, theoretical and practical, for alternative, human-scale means of producing the essential food, clothing and shelter. Like much of this chapter, a personal choice must be made of examples.

'For me,' wrote Gandhi, 'nothing in the political world is more important than the spinning wheel.' In his attempt to free the Indian peasant from the effects of industrialisation — in this case part of Britain's domination — he founded a spinning movement, raised funds to buy wheels for the villagers, to train spinning and weaving teachers and to open shops in which to sell the cloth. This income supplemented the poor farming yield. Gandhi calculated that the Indians could produce their own needs, thirteen yards of cloth a year each, from Indian cotton, then greatly exported raw to Japan and England. His own clothes, towels and sheets were home-made. And, to make the politicians conscious of the peasantry, he put the spinning wheel at the centre of the Congress Party flag, now that of India.

On a second plane, Gandhi called spinning 'a sacrament' turning the mind 'Godward'; he span each evening. His secretary, Pyarcelal, has said that, in the spinning wheel, Gandhi found 'rhythm, music, poetry, romance — even spiritual solace.'

Attempts to become independent of the industrial aspects of society have long been commonplace. One of the first to use solar energy alongside his grinding mill, weaving apparatus and other simple tools was Bill Propter. He had concluded, or rather his creator Aldous Huxley had done so, that 'the inhabitants of every civilised country are menaced; all desire passionately to be saved . . . the overwhelming majority refuse to change the habits of thought, feeling and action which are directly responsible for their present plight.' Reflecting on the lot of an exploited transient fruit-picker, once a farmer, he decides that: 'His gravest offence had been

to accept the world in which he found himself as normal, rational and right. Like all the others, he had allowed the advertisers to multiply his wants; he had learned to equate happiness with possessions, and prosperity with money to spend in a shop. Like all the others, he had abandoned any idea of subsistence farming to think exclusively in terms of a cash crop.'

Propter is asked, sceptically: 'Can't you believe in Jefferson and have your current wired in from the city?'

'That's exactly it,' he replies, 'you almost certainly can't.'

Elsewhere Huxley wrote that 'inventors and engineers should provide ordinary people with the means of doing profitable and intrinsically significant work . . . to achieve independence from bosses, so that they may become their own employers, or members of a self-governing co-operative group working for subsistence and a local market . . .,' leading to a 'progressive decentralisation of population, of accessibility of land, of ownership of the means of production, of political and economic power.'

These words could be used as part of the creed of the modern 'alternative technology' movement. Schumacher, creator of perhaps the best-known organisation, the Intermediate Technology Development Group, has proposed small-scale, easily-established non-violent technology, practised under creative conditions, within organisations under worker-owner management or under common ownership. Schumacher has added that 'Intermediate technology does not imply simply a 'going back' in history to methods now outdated, although a systematic study of methods employed in the developed countries, say, a hundred years ago could yield highly suggestive results.' Throughout the present book there will be found descriptions of almost-forgotten materials and techniques which may be usable as they stand or could be adapted to present needs by the craftsman and the intermediate technologist. Hand-spinning is technologically short of 'intermediate' at present. It is the author's opinion that the craft, especially if practised using an improved wheel — such as that made to the design offered in the last chapter — yields a result which makes the craft viable both for home-production and as a community trade.

Problems of the craftsman in alternative society

Right away it is necessary to outline various difficulties. Where Huxley and Schumacher have constructed wide-ranging alternatives to industrialised society, William Morris concentrated on a single facet: the heightening of life through a high level of art and craft, in his personal case of the two combined. Consideration of his opinions is thus particularly relevant — as is that of the contradictions which he met and which, now more than ever, face the modern craftsman.

Morris was born into a wealthy middle-class family in 1834. Influenced by Ruskin's pioneering of the social, educational and aesthetic qualities of handicrafts — leading to their first 'conscious' practice — Morris the socialist cried out despairingly: 'I do not want art for a few, any more than education for a few, or freedom for a few.' Steeped in the usually inseparable art-craft traditions of the Middle Ages, he wrote in 'Art & Democracy' on the craftsman's work: 'He was allowed to carry it through leisurely and thoughtfully; it used the whole of a man for the production of a piece of goods, and not small portions of many men; it developed the workmen's whole intelligence according to his capacity . . . , a system which 'supposed in its simplicity that commerce was made for men.' One of Morris's outstanding skills was as a designer and weaver of tapestries and other fabrics, these embellishing the houses of the wealthy bourgeoisie. From these various aspects of his life arose what can be called the 'Morris dichotomy', expressed one day in a Samson-like outburst whilst in a Victorian temple: 'I spend my life ministering to the swinish luxury of the rich,' he shouted. There was further conflict completely within his own life, between the lavish and exotic art he practised and his expressed preference for plain wood and whitewashed walls.

Morris's problems are still present. However, he did

advocate a different approach to that which he had himself followed. In 'The Decorative Arts: Their Relation to Modern Life and Progress,' of 1882, he proposed a return to functional simplicity, to such fundamentals as fitness for use. He also suggested, incidentally, that only those who led natural and unaffected lives would produce natural and unaffected work.

It may be that a craft is only truly alive if it has a practical role in the community. So long as a craftsman produces for a wealthy elite or turns out functionless art-apeing work because it fetches high prices, or works for tourism — an industry Morris did not have to watch in action — for just so long the craftsman remains chained to industrial society. The alternative way of Morris was the only way of Gandhi: in his alternative society the spinners and weavers put their craft — and art — into making the clothing, bedding and other essentials needed by their own community.

The life of the craftsman

A craftsman's day brings not only, again in Schumacher's words, 'the rarest privilege, the opportunity of working usefully, creatively, with his own hands and brains, in his own time, at his own pace . . . ', it both allows and brings about a different approach to life. One has only to glance back at Thorsrud's charge-list against industrial society to realise this.

There is of course a contradiction in consciously changing from mainstream society to Morris's 'natural unaffected life,' one eagerly seized upon by those fearful of the minority culture. Conscious destruction is accepted as inevitable and even as 'progress', but conscious reconstruction is 'artificial' and 'back to nature'. But a movement can anyway only be fairly judged by its results. Morris's group offered little to the majority because it was in fact a nostalgic, romantic revival of the Middle Ages. To be communally relevant, a movement must grow out of the lives of the community.

Inseparable from discussion of a modern craftsman's life is the appearance in the third quarter of the twentieth century of a myriad of small, varied communities. Conscious of themselves — as are most of those who live on government housing schemes, acceptable to majority society — they suspect that industrial man's life has been made the colder by its many divisions: into rigorously-vigilated individual territories, into work and leisure, into those with whom one works, with whom one plays, with whom one lives the rest of the time. 'During the long winter nights, from the dearness of the candle and their social disposition, they form what they call *cymmortheu gwau;* numbers assemble at each other's dwellings in rotation and sitting around a turf fire, pursue their wonted tasks, while tales of other times beguile the hours or the village harper thrums his dulcet tones . . . the hills . . . are covered with these people in the summer.' Not a modern commune but the spinners and knitters of the Welsh village of Bala, in 1804. Family life must have had a different texture: 'I remember waking one morning,' wrote Millet the painter (1814—75), recalling his earliest impressions, 'to a burring sound which kept stopping and starting . . . it was the noise of spinning wheels and with it came the voices of women carding wool.'

In a recent article, 'Communities: Example and Symbol', Haughton has written that, as the communitarian movement grows, so 'many of the things the communities do, and which were once considered freaky and ridiculous by most people (organic farming, trying 'alternative' sources of energy, group living as 'therapy' for people in trouble, eating less meat, sharing of certain responsibilities between families, renovating old building and many others) are more and more regarded as sensible things to do.' Referring to 'the state of moral disarray in which the older social groupings find themselves,' she suggests that 'hope (if any) lies in the grouping of people, including families, in small but efficient local groups, to help *themselves.'* Amongst the organisations expressing and crystallising the trend is the Communes Movement; deploring the individual's loss of 'the art of

10

1. *Woman carding, prepared wool in foreground, a hand-wheel behind. (J.F. Millet, 1814-75)*

providing himself with the basic necessities of life,' its aims can be found in its manifesto, 'A Federal Society based on the Free Commune.' If the new commune's way of life is in practice no more ideal than that of the old pre-industrial community, it does seem to many to provide a more satisfactory way of working and living, with greater promise for the future, than does industrial society.

CHAPTER 2

THE EARLY DEVELOPMENT OF HAND—SPINNING

'A knowledge of Industrial History has now become indispensable for every citizen who aspires to understand, and to participate in the solution of, the social and economic problems of his generation. For those actually engaged in an industry a knowledge of its history is a vital necessity. The importance of humanising industry, and restoring the medieval concept of it as public service . . .', these words have a relevant ring even half a century later. They are from the editor's preface to Lipson's *The Woollen and Worsted Industries* (1921) on the industrialisation of the wool trade.

Prehistoric origins

Diderot's *Encyclopédie,* about 1750, tells of a 'savage' who was brought to Paris and taken round a cloth workshop; unimpressed, he did try a blanket round his shoulders, then giving it back and saying, condescendingly: 'Well, it's almost as good as skin.' In spite of this informed opinion, cloth has advantages in use, such as elasticity, and in economy, in that it is not necessary to kill an animal to make it.

The most obviously available and, in many areas, the longest spinnable fibre is human hair (fig. 2). Possibly this was the first spun fibre; there are primitive peoples in the

12

2. *Human hair, x 1250, showing imbrications (author's excavation, c3000 BC, Scottish Mesolithic culture)*

Pacific and Australia whose limited spinning has been of human hair, often for use in ritual masks. Or the idea may have come from the natural twisting of wet vegetable fibre: the Neolithic Egyptians did spin flax in its natural direction. There were wild sheep and goats in the Middle East and their short coats may have been the inspiration source. In South America, spinning was either invented independently or received from Asia. In its first stage, the spinner needs no tools at all; most primitive groups have sooner or later used a weighted stick, as will be described in Chapter 8.

Neolithic culture first developed from about 10,000 BC in the Middle East, with domesticated sheep at Shanidar, in Iraq, by 9000, and goats at Catal Hüyük by 6500; animal fibre was thus acceleratingly available. The earliest

3. Spindle, c1370 BC, Egypt

13

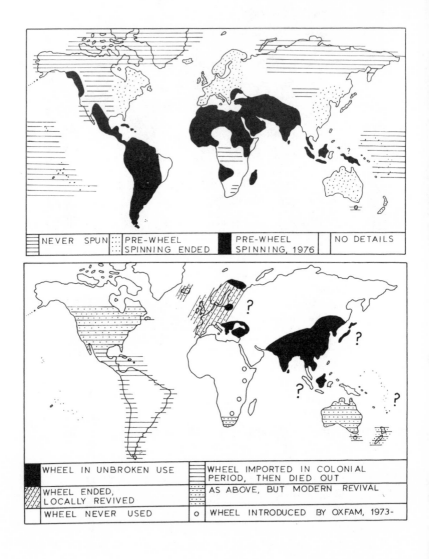

NEVER SPUN	PRE-WHEEL SPINNING ENDED	PRE-WHEEL SPINNING, 1976	NO DETAILS

WHEEL IN UNBROKEN USE		WHEEL IMPORTED IN COLONIAL PERIOD, THEN DIED OUT
WHEEL ENDED, LOCALLY REVIVED		AS ABOVE, BUT MODERN REVIVAL
WHEEL NEVER USED	o	WHEEL INTRODUCED BY OXFAM, 1973-

4. Maps. Upper: primitive native spinning
  Lower: advanced spinning, including colonists

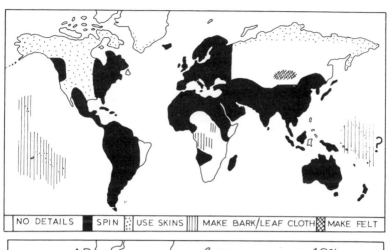

| NO DETAILS | ▇ SPIN | ⣿ USE SKINS | ‖‖‖ MAKE BARK/LEAF CLOTH | ▨ MAKE FELT |

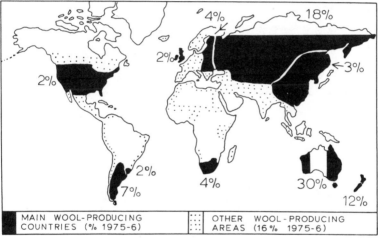

| ▇ MAIN WOOL-PRODUCING COUNTRIES (% 1975-6) | ⦂⦂⦂ OTHER WOOL-PRODUCING AREAS (16% 1975-6) |

5. Maps. Upper: pre-industrial native spinning, with main native fabric
elsewhere
Lower: distribution of the world's sheep

15

Table 1: Earliest known dates (BC) for spinning in different regions

Fibre	Middle East	Europe	Asia	America
Flax	6500: Turkey (Catal Hüyük) 5000: Egypt (Fayum)	3000: Switzerland (Lake Dwellings) 1000: Britain (Late Bronze Age)	2000: India (Mohenjo-Daro)	
Wool	As flax (above)	2000: Britain 1500: Denmark	500: USSR (Pazyryk) 500	BC: Peru
Hemp	4000: Egypt (Badarian)			
Cotton	500: Sudan (Meroë)		2500: India (Mohenjo-Daro)	2500: Peru, Mexico 500: USA pre-2300: ?Peru
Sisal				
Silk	1000: China (Yin)			
Nettle		800: Denmark		
Esparto	BC: Mesopotamia	BC: Spain		
Asbestos		BC: Italy		
Pinna			150 AD: India	
Fibre unknown		5000: Hungary (Körös) 3000: Britain (Neolithic)	2000: China (Yang-Shao)	

concrete evidence for spinning, in the world, is given in Table 1. Legends go back further: for example, silk in China to the Empress Si-Ling-Chi (c2640 BC), cotton in Peru to the legendary 'first' sovereign, Manco Copac. Body colourings now moved on from the surface of skin clothing into the spun fibres, the craft of dyeing. Weaving was invented: there is cloth from Catal Hüyük (6500), a loom is shown on a Fayum-culture dish (5000).

As is suggested by this chronology and distribution (fig. 4), spinning has developed unevenly in the world. People in very cold areas have instead used skin or felt clothes and tents, others in extremely hot regions have always gone naked or made light coverings without spun fibre (fig. 5). A wide variety of materials (Chapters 4,5) and of techniques, (Chapters 6–9) have been used by those who spun.

Dynastic, Biblical and Classical developments

Although there have always been male spinners — ranging from those in Egyptian dynastic drawings to present-day Salish Indians of British Columbia — spinning has usually been done by women, particularly amongst materially-advanced peoples. Jewish law enjoined that the virtuous woman 'seeketh wool and flax and worketh willingly with her hands', though 'married women should not spin in the street, nor in the open and certainly not by the light of the moon.' The commonness of the work, together with its particular association with unmarried women, has given English a common noun, 'spinster'; male textile workers, whose surnames are transmitted by marriage, have passed down 'Dyer', 'Fuller' and the names of other specialised cloth crafts.

Organisation has varied widely. If the Salish still spin for themselves in the nineteen seventies, Mesopotamian towns like Ur had their girls and women organised in factories several thousand years ago. The first known textile baron, 'Master-spinner Khety;' was buried with much

17

pomposity in a sumptuous eleventh dynasty tomb (embell-ished with fig. 22a) at Thebes, in Egypt, about 1900 BC.

Khety's employees were spinning flax, since the Egyptian bourgeoisie did not like wool, even for mummy cloth, and, as Moses noted, considered 'every shepherd an abomination.' Hebrew priests, too, were only to wear linen 'and no wool shall come upon them while they minister; they shall not gird themselves with anything that causeth sweat.'

By the fifth century BC, a 'tree wool,' cotton — presumably the arboreal species — was known in Egypt and the East Mediterranean: 'The trees of India bear fleeces,' said Herodotus, 'far surpassing those of sheep in beauty.' Cotton then spread slowly into south-east Europe, perhaps with hemp. Eastwards from India, cotton was known in China by at least 200 BC.

Silk reached the Near East in its late Iron Age, Ezekiel writing in the sixth century BC that 'Thus wast thou decked with gold and silver; and thy raiment was of fine linen, and silk, and broidered work.' The Romans were wearing imported silk in 200 BC but it took until 550 AD for the grubs themselves to be smuggled out of China to Constantinople, where, under Justinian, the first European silk was spun and woven. The Japanese had obtained Chinese silk-grubs by 300 AD and the Indians did so soon after.

Narrowing the focus to Britain — referred to, unless otherwise stated, for the rest of this book — its textile history opens about 700 BC with Phoenician traders exchanging woollen cloth for tin in Cornwall; raw wool was being exported about then, its amount probably increasing parallel to the development of sheep-rearing over the last millenium BC. This export-raw, import-woven pattern was due to the lack of weaving expertise amongst the British. Change occurred in the last centuries BC: Iron Age sites such as Glastonbury Lake Village had important woollen industries whilst either the Belgic immigrants or the Roman conquerors improved the British sheep. The large flocks supplied fleece to textile factories run by Roman *entrepreneurs* and colonial landowners and making the legionaries' uniforms; a new type of loom was introduced. At the time of Diocletian, third-fourth century AD, the finer wool was for home use, the coarser for capes and rugs for export. This organised period of the wool trade ended with the invasions of the Angles, Jutes and Saxons in the fourth and fifth centuries.

The historical role of the spinning wheel

The discoverers of all the main hand-spinning materials and techniques remain unknown. Much about the wheel is unclear. In the broadest terms, it was probably invented in China, Indochina or India, after 3000 BC, the maximum antiquity for spinning in Asia, and was much like the wheel (figs.6, 23a) still in use there today; without a treadle, it will be called the 'hand-wheel'. Similar wheels are current for reeling up the unwinding thread of silkworm cocoons and for filling weavers' bobbins with yarn, but which of the three uses came first is unknown. There is no sign of the hand-wheel in Europe until, without immediate provenance, it is abruptly recorded there in the late Middle Ages.

6. Chinese two-spindle hand-wheel

19

The earliest references were thirteenth-century German and French decrees limiting the use of the hand-wheel to weft-spinning, the primitive, weighted stick being preferred for the more demanding warp yarn for a further 200-500 years, according to region. In fact, its introduction was always opposed, generally on the grounds of inferior production but also because the rich feared the increased output would raise servants' wages, so that is spread only very slowly through Europe. During its first two or three centuries in the west it came into use not only in Germany and France but also in Austria, Holland and England; the first illustration of the hand-wheel is in fact in the Luttrell Psalter, about 1338. Outlying countries such as Scotland, Denmark and, probably, Norway and Sweden, had this wheel by 1600; Velasquez painted one, in 1658, in his 'Minerva and Arachne' (fig.7); two Shetlanders implanted it in the Faeroes in 1671.

These hand-wheels also came to be used in the region of southern Italy, Bulgaria and Cyprus, apparently surviving there today. This triangle may have been on the wheel's approach path to Europe. Had the region received these wheels from Europe, then it might be expected that the same carrier — probably trade — would in turn have brought the treadle wheel. However, these places were on the trade route from India. For example, Indian cotton had reached Europe by the late Middle Ages, perhaps impelled by the same force that led to cotton cloth being made in China from 1280; in one of the earliest references to its manufacture in England, in 1641, London was receiving bales of cotton direct from Cyprus.

It is not known to what degree the advent of the wheel stimulated the cloth trade of north-west Europe — developing by the thirteenth century — but it is clear that the evolution in textiles must have led to the improvements soon

8. Flax hand-wheel with earliest-known flyer, Waldburg, c 1480

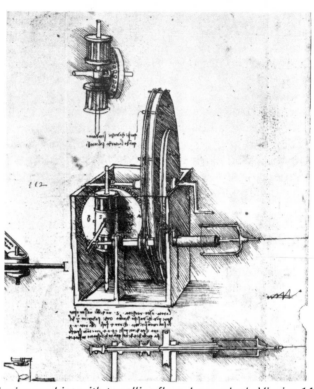

9. Spinning machine with travelling flyer, Leonardo da Vinci, c 1490

made to the wheel. Thus, by 1480, there was a German wheel with a flyer (fig.8), allowing much greater continuity of spinning; this was the most important invention since the idea of using the wheel in the craft (see Chapters 8,9 for technical discussion). About 1490, Leonardo sketched a device for spreading the spun yarn evenly on the bobbin (fig.9), more suited to a machine than to the simple wheel. The Glockendon Bible of 1524 is said to illustrate the second major invention, the treadle; or it may have been first made by J Jurgen of Brunswick in 1533. The flyer-treadle wheel allows an almost continuous spinning sequence from an empty to a full bobbin. The Chinese treadle wheel (fig.25d) is distinct, having no flyer and with a fulcrum treadle; the latter is said to have been added in the seventeenth century AD.

10. *Goat shepherdess with spindle and distaff, nineteenth century France (Millet)*

The improved or 'Saxony' wheel — technically indistinguishable from those used into this century (figs. 24-6) — slowly spread across Europe in the wake of the hand—wheel. Distant states such as Poland, Hungary and Russia to the east and Scotland, Wales and Ireland to the west were not using it until about 1700; Spain not until a century later. Iceland received its first wheels, some primitive and some advanced, in 1750.

In fact, the earlier spinning tools — the spindle and the hand-turned wheel — continued alongside the most sophisticated wheel, as Millet's drawings of about 1866 show (figs. 1,10). By this time the two wheels were also in use in those parts of Africa and America which, from at least 1600, had received colonists from Europe. Probably the world had its highest proportion of hand-spinners about 1750.

The textile craft in the late Middle Ages

The Normans' conquest once again took Britain into Europe, stimulating the export of high-quality raw wool to Flanders; the spreading monastic orders, notably the Cistercians from 1100, reared many of the large flocks which supplied the wool. The Flemish sent back cloth; Britain again lacked not only dyes and mordants but up-to-date craftsmen, its production only for home consumption. A medieval manuscript describes the Welsh, for example, as 'a people having a wide experience of woollen manufacturing but who paid no attention to industry or commerce.' However, unlike spinning, weaving was by now specialist work in most communities; a loom cost an appreciable amount. Lacking a large-scale textile trade, then, development centered around sheep breeding and the inter-action of grazing and tillage (Chapter 5). Wool's only competitor was then flax, grown and processed on a more limited scale. 'Cotton wool' had reached Europe by the thirteenth century as noted, but was only used for the wicks of candles in Britain. Silk was a luxury import.

This was a calm period in the British wool-crafts compared with that which followed — and with that which the more developed continental trade was already experiencing. The conflict went back to at least the time of Ur and Thebes and reached forward to the present day: the division between capital and labour. The late-Medieval battle of Courtrai was fought by the weavers in an attempt to gain a say in town affairs, independence of action and the right to form a union. As an example of the period's opponents to the emancipation of the craftsmen, there is Jehan Boyne Broke of Douai, a cloth-merchant who, in 1300, took over almost the whole town by the work-debt syndrome. He owned the buildings, rented out lodgings and looms to weavers whom he attracted by promises of adequate work; he then gave out only enough employment for them to pay the rent and barely survive, so they found themselves trapped. Naturally Boyne Broke owned lands on which he grew the only supplies of dye-plants and wool, these delivered only against completed work. Those who complained were given no more work at all. Alternatively there was revolt, no more successful. In 1371 the Cologne workers rose against their masters: 33 weavers were executed and as many as could be found less officially murdered, 1800 families were banished and the weavers' guild-hall destroyed.

The British cloth-trade began to develop in the fourteenth century and was soon the foremost industry in the country, a position held for four or five centuries. The State now encouraged the production and export of cloth but placed a high duty on outgoing raw wool. Simultaneously, and partially as a result, Flemish weaving began to decline. A first group of Flemish weavers, together with their techniques, was brought to Britain about 1330. Within Britain, the new duty ensured raw wool to the craftsmen and clothiers but angered the farmers, these used to the higher return abroad. Spain now began to supply raw wool to the rest of Europe. In Britain there was also opposition to the development of an export-based economy — a balance with tillage and fishing was advocated. The subsequent centuries of complex trade restrictions and duties, of the State's control and then of its loss of command to capitalism — these direct effects alone throw doubt on the wisdom of the fourteenth-century decision-makers.

The late-Medieval prosperity was celebrated at the great wool fairs or 'staples', meeting places of the workers and, as time went on, of the growing class of employers. The weavers had organised the first guild (Anglo-Saxon 'gild' or money) by the twelfth century, but, before describing this institution, the three-stage evolution of the textile trade, reaching to the present, can be summarised:

1) The guild system, effective until the seventeenth century, with the spinners, dyers and weavers working in their own premises, owning their tools and materials and selling their products first direct to the consumer and then, increasingly, to capitalist middlemen.

2) The domestic system, its ending ranging between 1600—1850 according to remoteness and the peculiar-

ities of each craft — now the workers had only their own premises and tools, being employed to process materials belonging to capital.

3) The factory system, in which the employees own nothing and the premises, tools and materials belong to the employers.

The medieval guild was built around a single craft in one town; membership was compulsory, with those who refused to join treated harshly and even on occasion killed. There were three basic classes: masters, journeymen and apprentices. The masters organised the craft; fixed prices and wages; transmitted the techniques personally; tried to suppress change, such as inventions, and to keep national and guild monopolies intact; settled disputes between members and between guilds, frequent when these were associated, for example those of each process in cloth-making ; enforced both material and moral standards. Amongst these last were that no craftsman should entice away another's customers nor should in any way seek unfair advantage over the other members, as by hoarding raw materials for re-sale at higher prices during scarcity.

The masters played the part of employers to the apprentices, these amongst the slaves of the period; this was accepted since the masters had first served the full apprenticeship, seven years, themselves. These boys were ruled not only in their work but as to place of residence, whether they could marry and so on. In fact, the apprentice, 'industrious' often contrasted with 'idle', was made into a 'good citizen' by the system, at a time when social responsibility was not formally discharged by simply paying rates and taxes. Once his indentures were ended, the apprentice became a journeyman: after a few years as a hired workman (by the *journée*, or day) he had saved enough money to buy, say, a loom, and acquired enough confidence to set up a workshop as a master.

The guild also had a wider practical role in society, again underlining that pre-industrial man did not live a compartmented existence. Thus, church and guild were linked. The guild looked after the poor amongst its members.

It also played its part in social life, particularly in organising festivals. Although the guilds' influence did not reach beyond the seventeenth century, the festivals themselves went on into the industrial age.

In 1825, for example, the Bradford wool-combers held a procession in honour of their patron saint, Blaize, done to death with iron combs in 316 AD. In front came a herald with a flag; then the wool-staplers, each draped in a fleece, on horseback; the worsted spinners in white-stuff sashes and waistcoats, a sliver over the shoulder, also on horses, the animals' necks covered with nets of thick yarn; behind them came the wool merchants, on horses, with coloured sashes; guards; the apprentices in caps ornamented with ostrich feathers, flowers and yarns, scarlet coats, white waistcoats and blue pantaloons; band; the mace-bearer, on foot; the wool-sorters in caps with plumes and with coloured slivers; the comb-makers, with combs on standards, golden fleeces and rams' heads; the charcoal burners; the wool-combers colours; bands; the combers themselves, in woollen wigs; the dyers with red cockades, blue aprons, crossed red and blue slivers; and all manner of general characters, such as a mock king and queen. Modern industry has replaced this by the works outing to the football match.

CHAPTER 3

INDUSTRIALISATION, 1500 AD ONWARDS

'And in another place hard by,
An hundred women merrily
Were carding hard with joyful cheer
Who singing sate with voices clear
And in a chamber close beside
Two hundred maidens did abide,
In petticoats of Stammell red,
And milk-white kerchiefs on their head
These pretty maids did never lin (stop)
But in that place all day did spin.'

Doubtless the sixteenth-century 'Pleasant History of John Winchcombe' was not penned by a worker for, when these found time to write doggerel, the 'joyful cheer' was missing. An example was the ballad of Charles II's time 'wherein is exprest the craftiness and subtility of many Clothiers in England in beating down their Workmen's wages,' with lines such as:

'The Tucker and Spinner that spin all the year,
We will make them earn their wages full dear.'

This was in fact the period in which the workers lost their medieval independence but were still far from gaining their modern rights: in which the State's decision-makers, placing more value on 'national' interests than on the well-being of those who made up the majority of the nation, took over the trade, only to have to relinquish it to capital; in which proto-industry invaded the home, school, prison and poor-house in its frenzied efforts to increase the number and output of the spinners, since profits depended directly on the supply of spun yarn.

It has been said that the guild craftsmen had begun to sell their products to clothiers by the end of the Middle Ages. By about 1500 these *entrepreneurs* had organised the smaller, often-seasonal craftsmen into the 'domestic-system' — contract work at home — and were making their first steps towards the 'factory system', as can be seen from the opening poem.

The further the clothiers extended their control of the cloth trade the richer they were becoming, so that during the sixteenth century they emerged as a wealthy middle-class, ranking between the aristocracy and the workers. Alongside them were the farmers who had become rich by supplying the wool. These two groups, initially only controlling each end, gradually took over all the textile processes, at length merging into one as the 'manufacturers.' Holding the wealth necessary to own the materials, the manufacturers at first moved the goods from home to home whilst, rising in value, these slowly approached the state of finished cloth. For the spinners a network of 'pack houses' was developed, places where raw wool and flax were left for them and to which they returned it once spun. This system was inefficient from the manufacturers' view-point since, as Morris would have put it, the craftsmen supposed in their simplicity that 'commerce was made for men' and not the other way about — and at harvest time, for example, gathered in their crops instead.

And so the successors to Jehan Boyne Broke moved on to the third stage: the factory. First, the workers were brought to live close together, so that inspectors could be sent round, bells could be rung for lunch and for the beginning and end of 'working hours'. Their ownership of the workers' houses and of the local shops also allowed the manufacturers to pay the wages in rent and goods at rates favourable to themselves, a 'truck' system (French *truquer,* to exchange) lasting, in spite of legislation, until a century ago. The 'gentleman-farmers', from their end, had their own wool prepared and spun by their labourers, the manors became increasingly organised 'manufactories' in the winter time. Then, inevitably, the first full-time factory building was opened, probably in the sixteenth century. This allowed not only control of the craftsmen but also of their techniques — the removal of their last independence of action. The master-craftsmen moved into the role of over-seers for the employers.

The craftsmen were not the only ones to suffer, for the profit-motive brought on the English clearances: 'Where have been a great many householders and inhabitants, there is not but a shepherd and his dog,' said Latimer, whilst Tyndale complained that 'God gave the earth to men to inhabit, and not unto sheep and wild deer.' The farm-labourers displaced by these clearances were amongst the first to move to the towns and work for the industry which had disrupted their lives. However, the manufacturers, as they gave work to so many, were much admired as philanthropists, at least by those of their own society.

Children, convicts and the destitute are put to spin

Particularly admirable were felt to be the spinning 'schools', set up right across Europe between 1600 and 1750. These were simply factories, aiming at a maximum output of standardised yarns, to which the manufacturers, hitherto not noted for their contribution to education, consigned the children of the poor. A German school of 1685 was for 'little Girls, six years old . . . to bring their tender fingers by degrees to spin very fine; their Wheels go all by the Foot . . . with much ease . . . upon the benches sit about two hundred Children spinning, and in the box in the middle . . . sits the grand mistress with a long white Wand . . . if she observe any of them idle, she reaches them a tap, but if that will not do, she rings a bell . . . and out comes a Woman, she then points to the Offendor . . . she is taken away into another Room and chastized; and all this done without one word.' Then 'In a little Room . . . a woman . . . is preparing and putting Flax on the distaffs, and upon the ringing of a Bell, and pointing the rod at the maid that hath spun off her flax, she hath another Distaff given her.' Although spinning is quickly learned, the child went on indefinitely at the 'school', her minute pay ensuring that 'in these parts . . .a man that has most Children, lives best.' The various results of the system can be imagined.

In 1661, legislation establishing linen-making as a Scottish industry also brought with it the decision that there should be instruction of 'the poore childreen vagabonds and other idlers to fine and mix wooll, spin worsted and knit stockings'; about 1727 the 'schools' were introduced into the Highlands. Welsh children were given over to the industry from 1756. The manufacturers offered prizes for spinning at the county agricultural shows.

The British were pioneers of the 'corrective workshop'; one of the first was at Winchester where, in 1578, the women prisoners were made to spin and knit. In 1605 the idea was copied, from the Scots, by the Danes, together with the hand-turned wheel; the women were known as 'Scottish -wheel women', so that this model was never used by Danish society because of its associations. Alongside this prison workshop, soon current throughout Europe, was the 'workhouse': the destitute of any age or sex could earn a very low wage there by spinning for industry. Many penal workshops and poor people's workhouses were actually set up by capitalists in agreement with city authorities. The idea of easily-obtainable work for the community is not in question here, but rather the exploitation of the more or less defenceless workers by the manufacturers, as demoralising perhaps as the workless dole of the extreme 'welfare state.'

Nevertheless there was still not enough yarn — there could never be — especially once, in 1733, Kay invented the flying shuttle. Until about then it had been said that 3—4 spinners were needed to supply a weaver; by 1700, 4—6 spinners are mentioned as the figure — the weavers too were under pressure to produce more and more. Thus there were states where taxes could be paid in spun wool and others where girls who did not learn to spin could not take communion nor marry. Prussia introduced spinning sessions into the army. Yet the wages continued low: it was officially possible, again in Prussia, to be both a spinner and a certified beggar.

The last and most universally applied innovation of the manufacturers was the check or jack reel (figs.11,27), the device which, measuring the spinner's output, must have come to be the symbol of their slavery. The spun wool was wound round its arms, their circumference fixed exactly; a set number of turns produced a hank of a fixed length. And, epitomising the English State's changing attitude to the workers, there was a law to enforce the use of the reel.

11. Click reel for flax, Scotland, 1769

The State's changing approach to the trade

Put simply, between 1500-1750 the State came gradually to see profit, partially 'the nation's' and partially that sought by the textile manufacturers' lobby, as more important than human welfare. Laws proliferated, ordering, forbidding, taxing . . . all over the age of seven were to wear a woollen cap when out of doors, enjoined Elizabeth I — perhaps the first step towards a society dependent on personally-unnecessary consumption — and women must wear flannel next to the skin, an injunction of Charles II. Not even the dead could escape this king's laws, for a corpse was not to be 'put in, wound, or wrapt up, or Buried, in any Shirt, Shift, Sheet or Shroud, or anything whatever made or mingled, with Flax, Hemp, Silk, Hair, gold or silver, or other than what is made of sheep's wool,' with the same restrictions on the coffin lining; the 1661 decision to back the Scottish linen trade meant that all Scots had to go to rest in linen. The British public was thus forced to support the manufacturers and the export trade.

In addition, the State manipulated the labour market to the benefit of the textile industry. Thus in the sixteenth century it encouraged the further immigration of Protestant weavers, now fleeing religious persecution on the continent, since they had techniques lacking in Britain; this of course hit the British craftsmen. Normally, however, the State participated in the European practice of restricting the movement of skilled workers from country to country; those who fled, because both wages and laws were becoming increasingly onerous, had prices put on their heads. The French sent fugitive workers to the galleys, the Venetians preferred to poision their runaway craftsmen.

The clothiers were protected against foreign competition by the multiplying laws. The prohibitive duty on the export of raw wool led to much cross-Channel smuggling. In the second half of the seventeenth century the English manufacturers found they were being undercut, on the continent, by the Irish — due to their spinners' more extreme enslavement, in fact — and so in 1698 they had a law passed that Ireland's cloth should only go to England and Wales. The Irish weavers thereupon began to emigrate, only to find the same law then passed against cloth exported from the British colonies. The East India Company, sending silk and cotton cloth to Britain from about 1700, saw these legally refused admission from 1720.

The textile trade, the first to attract State legislation to any extent, was now enmeshed in about 300 laws. In 1750 it provided half the country's exports. However, lack of competition together with the other insidious effects of its peculiar evolution had by now led the trade into stagnation; it was weighed down by a wide range of unproductive profit-takers; protection was increasingly difficult in the 'free trade' climate then developing in Europe. This was the economic backdrop against which the current phase — workers against employers and machines — began to develop.

Inventions and new materials

Following the normal practice of the guilds, in Elizabeth I's reign the Drapers Company gave a man 20 shillings to suppress his fulling machine. Devices which put men out of work were not wanted, though it can be noted that those which killed them, weapons, were always accept-able. But the State, pursuing its new goal, profit, was by then encouraging the 'inventor', thus putting him amongst the elite, the forerunner of the 'scientist'. The patent system was developing by the fifteenth century in Venice. Both Leonardo da Vinci and, in the seventeenth century, Giovanni Branca, designed power-driven spinning machines.

The first craft to be affected was hand-knitting, closely associated with spinning. It was first practised in Peru, Arabia and Scandinavia, in various forms, in the last millenium BC. This hand-craft was gradually replaced by a machine put into use as early as 1589.

The first cotton-cloth — a fustian, of cotton weft on a flax warp — was made in 1641; at first the spinners and weavers bought the raw cotton and owned the finished cloth but within a century they too had become piece-workers for the manufacturers. In 1664 Robert Hooke suggested man-made fibre. A silk-weaving mill opened in 1718. From the workers' point of view, the richer European classes' increasing demand for a smooth wool cloth, 'worsted', was an advantage: it demanded five times as much work as a 'woollen', together with greater skill. To the manufacturers, worsted meant the same wool could be made to yield a higher profit, to the nation the same pasturage ultimately led to higher exports.

The State loses control to the manufacturers

The Civil War destroyed the power of the English monarchy and, from the end of the seventeenth century, parliament came markedly under the influence of the manufacturers. Until then the State had continued some of the guild functions which supported labour, for example by comply-ing with the craftsmen's requests for the fixing of fair wages; it had also been against the nascent factories, fearing the concentration of unruly workers. Henceforth it was to con-centrate on 'national profit' through exports.

The manufacturers were now demanding 'industrial freedom', saying it was repugnant 'to the liberties of a free people and the interest of trade that any law should super-sede a private contract honourably made between a master and his workmen.' The last wage-fixing statutes were ignored: 'The weavers by this Act will be rendered more our masters than we are now theirs. A levelling and turbulent spirit . . . ought never to be countenanced amongst the common people'. Once forced to provide for their redundant workers, the manufacturers' responsibility was now trans-ferred to the degrading Poor Law system; employing all and sundry in order to pay the minimum, the trade's standards fell; the aulnager, a medieval civil servant who watched the quality of the cloth, disappeared in 1724. The majority of the Tudor laws protecting the workers were repealed in 1809.

Had the manufacturers been less grimly intent on

profit they too might have held festivals to celebrate their form of mastery of the trade. The sumptuous procession would have been headed by an image of their patron saint, Adam Smith, the apostle of free trade. But their banner-cry was only a partial statement of Smith's philosophy and had the image miraculously spoken, his further opinions might have been heard: 'Those who feed, clothe and lodge the whole body of the people should . . . themselves be tolerably well fed, clothed and lodged . . . our merchants complain much of the effect of high wages . . . they are silent with respect to the pernicious effects of their own gains'.

The first combinations of workers

The most independently-minded of the textile craftsmen were the wool-combers. Traditionally single men, they worked wherever wages were best, as 'The Song of the Rambling Wool-Combers' shows. Wherever they were at work they had a bench on which their fellows 'on the tramp', in search of work, could rest; those who had to go on were given a penny from a common fund when they left. This 'combination', a nascent union, preferred to support its members in idleness rather than see them take low wages; they downed combs if another craftsman were ill-treated. Eventually membership certificates were issued.

It is not necessary to describe the subsequent development of the trades' union movement in Britain. The textile craftsmen's combinations suffered legal suppression, by the 1726 law, for example, and their members shared in the physical conflict with the police, as when in 1752 a thousand weavers attacked a Bradford prison and released thirty of their fellows. In 1806 a union was formed to raise wages, to regulate their part of the trade and — here it continued from the medieval guild — to resist the machines.

'What 20,000 men did, now 20 men can do'

Each invention was the work of several men. The profit from the evolution of one process was the stimulus to invention in another. English designs were the most advanced and many machines were smuggled abroad to be copied.

Between 1730—58, contemporary with the flying shuttle's advent and thus with a great increase in weaving speed, Paul, together with Bourn and Wyatt, designed and built the first working carding and spinning machines (figs. 18e, 22d), the latter donkey-driven: the essence of each patent was 'rowlers', toothed rollers to prepare the fibres, paired rollers to spin them. The latter rollers turned at different speeds so that the fibres, passing through them, from one to another pair, were stretched out to the desired thinness, then being spun as on an advanced wheel. From the hand-spinner's view-point, it was only too appropriate that Paul was a shroud-maker by profession.

The essential aspects of these machines, never widely used, were developed by Arkwright. Between 1769—75 he patented a carding machine (fig.13), a 'drawing' frame (fig. 22e), which gave the fibres a preliminary thinning and light twist and, thirdly, a horse-driven roller-based machine which spun the 'slubbing' on four spindles at once (fig.12). This last is clearly based on the Saxony hand-spinning wheel, like Paul's machine. A second version, using eight spindles, was water-powered and became known as a 'water-frame'.

In 1767, a little before Arkwright's machines appeared, Hargreaves designed his form of spinning engine, or 'jenny' (fig.14). A row of spindles was turned by a single man, upon whose strength and judgement the work still depended. The jenny can thus be classed as 'intermediate technology.' It was based on the primitive hand-turned spinning wheel.

The main features of the water-frame and of the jenny were crossed by Crompton to produce his 'mule' by 1779. The first wool-combing machine was designed, in 1789, by Cartwright, a trifling blow to the world's craftsmen compared to his main invention, in 1785: the power loom, drawing on Watt's recent invention of the steam engine.

12. Arkwright's spinning machine, 1769

13. Arkwright's carding machine, 1775

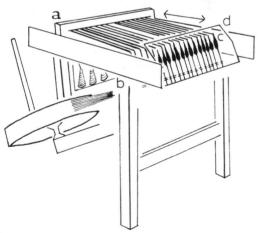

14. Hargreaves' spinning engine, simplified

In 1789, with doubtless unintentional irony, the French inventor Vay was able to say of the spinning mill that 'what 20,000 men did, now 20 men can do honestly in the same time.' The French workers attacked the rich class but the English craftsmen tried to improve their lot by an onslaught on the machines . . . in fact, the non-manufacturing gentry also initially feared the mechanical invasion, realising that it would increase their Poor Rate contribution. It was clearly understood by all groups that the machines would lead to unemployment yet, as always, the inventor-scientists not only continued their work uninhibitedly but actually received State encouragement.

The industrial system

The early factories had still required the workers to be craftsmen. Now they became 'semi-skilled' machine-users — still employing a degree of human ability and judgement — and, soon, merely 'unskilled' machine-minders. Visiting Bradford late in the nineteenth century, Morris noted that 'all the spinning and weaving is done by the women and children; the latter go to the mill at 10 years old as half-timers'. Women and children were cheaper and, no doubt, less militant. By coincidence, spinning 'schools' now ended. However, from 1780 what could be called 'carding schools' took their places. In 1830 a report spoke of the 'great hardships endured by the children . . . who joined the cardings . . . the piecer stood behind the billy . . . joining fresh lengths . . . This required constant watchfulness and great activity of the fingers . . . for twelve, fourteen and even sixteen hours a day . . . the skin was rasped off the fingers . . . if by any mischance they failed to piece one of the rolls, and thus caused an interruption of the work of the 'slubber', they were severely punished'. This work was ended in 1844, not by State action — although from 1830 there was the official report that the Bradford children were mentally and physically deformed as a result — but by the invention of a 'piecener' machine, doubtless more profitable still.

The fittest amongst the boys survived to be transformed by industry into a new middle-class of managerial and technical experts, taking up their new social positions amongst the cast-off chrysalises of the old manufacturers. These had grown so rich as to be now in turn shaking out their glittering new wings in the faces of the lower ranks of the unappreciative aristocracy.

The textile industry itself — henceforth increasingly treated, like the State, as an entity in itself, to be served for its own sake, a fiction half-consciously developed by capital ever since — has had a patchwork history over its subsequent 150 years. The first to be made mechanically, Yorkshire wool and Lancashire cotton cloths initially monopolised the world's markets. Cotton, first imported in large amounts in 1748, from North America, was found the easiest to mechanise, overtaking wool for cloth about 1800 and leading the trade ever since. Flax, not put into mechanical production until 1824, was badly hit by the development of the other two fibres. In 1833 a jute-spinning machine was designed and this Indian fibre was henceforth imported in quantity.

By 1800 the booming wool trade was short of raw fleece, so the farmers had to bow to omnipotent industry and see supplies brought from abroad, from Spain until 1818, then from the British colonies. The import figures (in millions of pounds weight), evenly spaced in time, give an idea of the effect of the machines:

1790: 2½m.lbs   *1850: 72½m.lbs*   *1907: 393m.lbs*

However, early in the nineteenth century, Britain's textile trade found itself hit by the spread of the machines to other countries, this gradually reducing the industry's internal and world importance. The smaller less-adaptable factories have been closing down, throughout Britain, since about 1830: no lament has been found for 'brave Newtown,' the fullness gone from its flannel by the end of the century. In 1884, Chardonnet produced the first man-made fibre, ultimately resulting in still further disruption and unemployment in the world's rural areas.

Britain still produces the most wool textiles in Europe, though it only sends 5% abroad. A tenth of the working population is in the industry.

If this history has been carried more or less into the memory of present society, it is to show how much of modern life is the result not only of industry's development but of that of the textile trade in particular. If the worker, now with a union, is in Britain at least usually 'tolerably well fed, clothed and housed', against this there is still Thorsrud's catalogue of the ills of industrial work, together with the adverse effects of industry on society in general, each discussed in the opening chapter.

Robert Owen, 1771—1858

It seems appropriate to place Owen here, in the turbid main-stream of textile history, rather than amongst the pure springs which characterise the opening pages of this book — since he combined his work for industrial reform and a better society with the role of Britain's leading cotton spinner. Owen's similar background and apprenticeship allowed him to work directly with the people as individuals: his schemes were thus relevant and practical, springing as they did from an understanding of the needs of the community.

In 1800, already famous, Owen took over the New Lanark cotton factory, in southern Scotland; Arkwright had been amongst its founders, as it happened. There were 2000 workers, a quarter of them poorhouse children, living at a low level materially and in spirit. Owen had already the expressed tenet that the subordination of man to machine would be a permanent cause of suffering. He reorganised the factory along humanitarian lines, including shorter working hours; he set up cheap shops and improved the workers' houses. All children were given education, the smallest in Britain's first infant schools. New Lanark became discussed right across Europe, often with admiration — though not, of course, with emulation. Yet the workers were said to be contented, the children transformed rather than, as in contemporary Bradford, deformed. And the mill was *still* commercially successful.

From here Owen went on, in 1817, to the first clear statement of socialist principles. He now founded the co-operative movement and a labour exchange which cut out profit-takers between those seeking and those offering work.

Owen's humanitarianism centered around his belief that the community was the lowest possible sub-division of a tolerable society. Thus his work for paupers was combined with the establishment of communal housing schemes; work and leisure were seen as community activities; he felt the children should be brought up in a communal environment. He founded communes in both Britain and America.

As Owen's life closed so did many of the practical schemes based on his beliefs die too. Yet, clearly enough, his ideas can be traced through to the present. Some have become universal principles, now as undoubted as they were 'reviled, and mocked, and feared' at the time. A few such as material comfort, have become exaggerated, even into ends in themselves, as much by labour as by capital. Others are still treated as absurd or at best impractical eccentricities. One of Owen's main goals, the small-community society, Haughton's 'only hope', becomes less and less attainable.

Epilogue: the last hand-spinners

The spinners, due to women's role in past society, lacked organisation and were the least able to resist each successive deterioration in the craftsman's position. True, about 1785 an unknown inventor added a second spindle assembly to the European wheel, also proposed by da Vinci, in an attempt to compete with the machines; on this wheel, used for about a century, a dexterous spinner could produce two threads at once, though each took much longer so that the yield only went up about a quarter. Much hand-spinning was carried on in the remoter farmhouses of Europe up to about 1900, the hired women having to do a stint each evening.

The spindle and distaff were still used a century ago in France (fig.10) and as recently as 1937 in South Uist in the Hebrides. About 1900, wheels turned by hand were still spinning in the Faeroes — worked by men, these having taken over from the women and their spindles several centuries previously — and in Wales. The Norwegians used the hand-wheel up to 1940. It is said to be still in use in west Eire; the west of northern Ireland uses the treadle wheel at present (an exception to fig.4, lower).

In Great Britain, hand-spinning survived longest in the Scottish mountains and islands. Offering few raw materials or profitable factory sites, their isolated communities were spared the initial onslaught of industrialisation. However, the manufacturers' demand for wool and the richer class's general demand for deer-shooting led, in remote Scotland, to human clearances comparable to those suffered by England in the proto-industrial period. The peasants' position was all the worse for many having become dependent on industry — through their landowners — as the purchaser of a crude fibre-cleanser which they made by burning seaweeds . . . industry itself abruptly replaced this by a chemical process about 1830. Simultaneously, agricultural reforms in the rest of Scotland were making farmwork continuous around the year, reducing the time for crafts. Thirdly, the country people were acquiring a taste for the machine-made clothing from the south and gradually worked less at crafts even for themselves.

Within remote Scotland, the crafts were most slowly affected in the islands. Just before it disappeared, a place was found for the Hebrides' cloth in the developing mythology of the southern sportsmen and tourists. The manufacture of this woollen twill, accidentally named 'tweed', had in fact been introduced to these communities by their gentry in the previous century, together with the spinning workshops for children. It now became fashionable to replace one's smooth worsteds by rough tweeds, together with a conspicuous 'deer-stalker' hat, before catching the Flying Scot northwards.

On the mainland, tweed cloth was being woven in

quantity by machinery by 1820 but in the Outer Hebrides it is still made on hand-looms with flying shuttles; in 1976 the weavers rejected industry's proposal to mechanise their work. The women of Lewis spun for their weavers until 1930, those of Harris are only ending now, in each case giving way to island or mainland machinery. The spinning and knitting of stockings was common into this century and the last Jura wheel, given to the author, was finally used between the world wars. In the Shetlands the last spinners spun for the shawl-knitters, these still at work.

CHAPTER 4

A SURVEY OF RAW MATERIALS

To be spinnable, a bundle of fibres needs to be capable of retaining the twist once the turning force has been removed. An animal hair, for example, is regularly surfaced with scaly imbrications — it is snake-like under the microscope (fig.2) — and these snag into those on adjacent hairs so as to maintain the spun position of the bundle. Vegetable fibres, though perhaps helped in some cases, such as ramie, by well-developed imbrications, retain the twist by moulding themselves readily into the new spiral position; moisture helps this, with flax, for example, twisting itself when damped.

The world's main yarn fibres are given in tables 2—3, together with some of the lesser-known European materials; a great many non-European vegetable fibres have had to be omitted. Table 1 gave the minimum antiquity of the most important fibres as yarns.

A fibre's main intrinsic qualities, apart from its spinnability, are its length, thickness, strength, elasticity, durability, warmth, natural colour and ability to take dye. Animal fibres are elastic and warm, averagely strong and durable; vegetable fibres are inelastic, cool and, in some cases, very strong and durable; artificial yarns are usually the strongest and most durable of all but make poor clothing and, more subjectively, are generally visually unattractive.

Range of breaking strains, starting with the strongest on the scale: ramie 8–5, flax 8–3, abaca 7½–6, hemp 7–6, cotton 6–3, jute 6–3, silk 6–3, wool 2–1.

Animal fibre is not easily obtained and is thus costly; much is imported into the industrial countries, a good part to be wasted in the luxury market and in over-consumption. Vegetable fibres are more easily produced and in Europe they are especially cheap since the growers are mostly in eastern countries and are paid low wages. Artificial fibres are also extremely cheap.

As Gandhi saw, this exploitation-dependency syndrome would be better replaced by reduced needs and self-sufficiency. Attempts at raising different fibre-yielding animals and plants in industrial regions 'fail' because mechanisation is yet again the means and commercial profit the end — whereas animals, plants and fibres respond best to individual attention and treatment.

Animal fibres

Most, perhaps all, of the fibre-yielding animals have two layers of coat. Usually a soft short furry inner grows amongst a harsher long hairy outer (Table 2: a,b).

The sheep and the goat are closely related, and, in fact, have almost indistinguishable skeletons. Sheep and their wool, the most important animal fibre in terms of world consumption, are left to the next chapter. The ancestor of the domestic goat was probably the bezoar, *Capra hircus aegagrus,* still wild in the high mountains of Central Asia; it has short greyish-brown hair with a black line along the back. The Tibetan and Angoran goats are domesticated types. The sheep-like Angora, an exceptional fleece known of 15 lbs, comes from Enguri in Turkey; it is said that all animals there have fine silky coats, losing them if taken elsewhere.

Camel's wool was presumably first spun in Asia, the

Table 2: Animal Fibres

Animal	Species	Fibre length	Fibre diameter	Weight of fleece	Colour	Special qualities	Main uses	Distribution of species
Man	Homo sapiens	< 6 ft	35-70mc	Small	White, yellow, red, grey, brown, black		Ritual masks	Wide
Sheep	Ovis aries	1-13"	15-45mc limits 10-90mc	< 35lb	White, brown, grey, black		Clothing, blankets, carpets	Wide. See Ch.5
Common Goat	Capra hircus	4-6"	a: 15mc b: 100mc	2 lb	White, fawn, brown, grey, black	Coarse, strong, springy	Carpets, tents	Wide
Angora Goat	Capra hircus	a: 4-6" b: < 10"	25-55mc	2½-5lb	White, red, black	a: coarser b: soft, lustrous	'Mohair' a: rugs, furnishings b: clothing	Turkey, S. Africa, USA, Fiji, Australia
Tibetan Goat	Capra hircus	a: 1¼-3" b: < 5"	15mc	¼-½lb (a)	Grey-white, brown	a: soft, silky b: coarser	'Cashmere' & 'Paisley' shawls	Tibet, Kashmir, China, Persia, Mongolia, Iraq
Camel	Camelus bactrianus C. dromedarius	a: 1½-2½" b: < 15"	a: 10-30mc	5lb	Yellow, brown		Clothing, tents	China, Mongolia, USSR. Arabia, N. Africa
Llama	Lama glama	5-10"	< 60mc		White, brown, black		Cloth, hats, bags, ropes	West and south of S. America
Alpaca	Lama pacos	8-12"	27mc	6lb	White, brown, grey, black	Fine, lustrous	Clothing, blankets	As llama
Guanaco	Lama guanicoe	Long	19mc		White, fawn	Fine, soft		Also wild. Area as llama

Animal	Species	Fibre length	Fibre diameter	Weight of fleece	Colour	Special qualities	Main uses	Distribution of species
Vicuña	Lama vicugna	1-2"	13mc	1 lb	White, reddish-yellow	Fine, soft	Shawls, knitwear, felt	Wild only. Area as llama
Angora Rabbit	Lepus cuniculus	a: 2½-3" b: < 7"	13mc	Small	White most valued	Fine, soft	Felt hats	Europe, Asia USA
Yak	Bos grunniens	Long			White, black	Soft		Asia
Bison	Bison bison				Brown		Cloth, hats	N. America
Musk Ox	Ovibos moschatus	a: short b: long			Brown	a: fine	a: scarves	N. America (Eskimos)
Dog	Canis familiaris				White			W. Canada (Indians)
Mink	Lutreola l., L. vison	Two coats			Dark brown to black	Soft		E. Europe N. America
Beaver	Castor fiber C. canadensis	Two coats			a: grey b: reddish-brown	a: silky b: coarser		E. Europe Canada
Raccoon	Procyon lotor P. cancrivorus	Long			Grey-brown	Coarse		N. America S. America
Silk Moth	Bombyx mori	330-900yd 4000yd	33-36mc by 20-25mc		Golden-yellow, white			China, Japan, India
Pinna Shell	Pinna nobilis				Cinnamon, gold		Stockings, gloves	S. Italy & isles India

Table 3: Vegetable Fibres

Vegetable	Species	Fibre type	Characteristics	Uses	Distribution
Flax	Linum usitatissimum	Bast	Fine, strong, smooth, repels water & dirt, inelastic. White to brown. Fibre length 8-45", diameter 16-20mc, limits 12-25mc	Clothing, sheets, canvas, cording	USSR, Europe
Cotton	Gossypium herbaceum, G.barbadensis G.hirsutum etc.	Seed hairs	Fine, soft, cool, absorbent. Cream to caramel. Fibre length 3/8"-2½" diameter 11-19mc	Clothing, sheets, furnishings, cording	India, America, Egypt China. Mallow family
Hemp	Cannabis sativa	Bast	Strong, water-resisting, inelastic. Fibre length 6-10', diameter 13-18mc	Clothing, sheets, canvas, cording	Asia, Europe, Africa, USA, Many pseudo-hemps
Jute	Corchorus capsularis, C. olitorius	Bast	Silky, easy to dye, soft, weak, rot-prone, coarse. Yellow-brown. Fibre length 6-7, up to 14'	Sacking, linings, cording	India, China, USA. Lime family
Abaca	Musa textilis etc.	Leaf	Strong, durable. Brown. Fibre length 3-9'	'Manilla hemp' Cording	Philippines. Banana family
Ramie	Bohmeria nivea etc.	Bast	Silky, strong, water-resistant, hard, inelastic, light, easy to dye. White. Fibre length 6" diameter 25-75mc	Nets, cording	China, India, Japan Nettle family
Sisal	Agave fourcroydes, A. sisalana	Leaf	Strong, coarse, rot-prone. White, cream. Fibre length 3-5'	Sacking, cording, hammocks	America, E. Africa, Indonesia, Canaries
Nettle	Urtica dioica, U. urens	Bast		Cording	N.Europe, N. Asia
Esparto	Stipa junceum	Leaf		Clothing, sheets, shoes, cording, mats, bags	Right around Mediterranean

Vegetable	Species	Fibre type	Characteristics	Uses	Distribution
New Zealand Flax	Phormium tenax	Leaf	Silky, strong. Cream Fibre length over 5'	Cloaks, mats, cording	New Zealand, Azores, S. America
Coir	Cocos nucifera	Nut exterior	Durable. Treated like bast	Cording, mats	Tropical, inc. Ceylon
Palm	Many spp.	Bast		Cording, mats	Wide
Spruce	Abies excelsa A. alba	Root		Cording	Lapland, Bothnia Canada
Fir	Pinus sylvestris	Bast Needles Root	Warm, durable, like coarse wool 'Like manilla hemp'	Cording Clothing, blankets Cording	Scandinavia, USSR Germany. Sweden Highland Scotland
Elm	Ulmus campestris	Bast		Cording, mats	Europe
Lime	Tilia europea	Bast		Cording, mats, bags	Europe
Sack Tree	Antiaris saccidora	Bast		Sacks	Ceylon
Common Mallow	Malva sylvestris	Bast		Cloth, shawls	Spain
Kenaf	Hibiscus cannabinus	Bast	Similar to jute. Fibre length 3-4'	Called 'hemp'	India A mallow
Seaweeds	Many spp.		Dissolve easily, flame-proof blood-clotting	Strengthen fine wool during weaving, then dissolved out. Dressings and tooth plugs	Wide

51

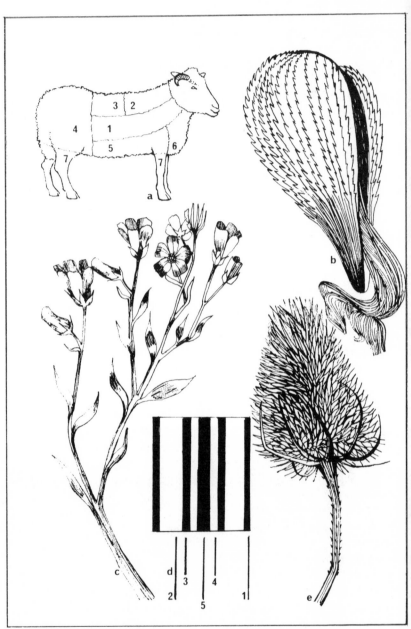

15. Raw materials: sheep fleece, according to quantities (a), pinna
mollusc (b), flax, with section through stem (cd), teazle thistle (e)

home of the bactrian and dromedary; the latter was taken to Africa by the first century BC. Related are the guanaco and vicuña of the high Andes of South America, the former now both wild and domesticated, the latter wild only. The vicuña has been hunted almost out of existence for its wool; the Incas decreed that the guanaco and vicuña should be chased only once every four years, the wool of the latter being reserved entirely for themselves and their court. Earlier, during the Peruvian Neolithic, the guanaco and vicuña had been domesticated, their well-evolved descendants being now, respectively, the llama, kept for meat and for transport as well as for wool, and the alpaca. There are also llama-alpaca crosses called *huarizo* and *misti.*

It was in 1836 that 'Mr. (now Sir) Titus Salt, a wool-broker and manufacturer in Bradford, purchased a quantity he met with in a Liverpool warehouse' making, in the words of the Victorian *Encyclopaedia Britannica,* 'alpaca a staple second . . . to wool . . . his experiments led . . . to his great manufacturing establishment of Saltaire, in which . . . 3000 hands are employed in the alpaca manufacture'. Attempts to rear the alpaca in Britain have always been described as failures; in 1976 a British woollen manufacturer is trying to raise llamas and alpacas on the Pennine moors.

Next come a class of large animals whose coats have usually only been spun incidentally: wild bison and musk oxen, domesticated cattle and horses. Then a group of small species, usually skinned rather than shorn: mink, beaver, raccoon. The very shortest of wool comes from rabbits and hares. Members of all three classes have provided fibre for felt-making; especially, in various combinations, cow, beaver, rabbit and hare.

The silk-moth is in its own peculiar class, the fibre coming from the cocoon made by the grub. Many wild species give silk, such as the tusseh (*Antheroea pernyi*); in Asia and *Tropoea luna* in the south of North America. The grub of the main domesticated species, *Bombyx mori*, ejects two flat filaments simultaneously from spinnarets on each side of its head: laid edge to edge, this four thousand yard ribbon is wound round itself by the grub like a loose mummy

53

bandage, to be laboriously unwound by the silk-worker once it has finished. Silk is two-thirds fibroin, thus being in fact comparable to wool. The silk-moth has never been successfully reared, from an industrial point of view, in the west, other than in Italy.

'Fleeces are obtained from the sea, where shells of extraordinary size are furnished with tufts of mossy hair', wrote the Roman Tertullian, in the second century AD, of the pinna industry, probably then in south India. Another theologian, Basil, in the fourth century recorded 'the golden fleece of the pinna, which no artificial dye can imitate.' In the early nineteenth century, divers for *lana pesce* were active around Sicily, Sardinia and Corsica, with the processing industry at Taranto in South Italy. The shell (fig. 15b), eighteen inches long, may originally have been collected for pearls. Its attachment to the sea-bed, a bundle of fine brown threads — zoologically called a 'byssus', from the Greek for a fine silky linen of the classical Mediterranean — was prepared with a bone comb and then spun and knitted into soft, warm, costly stockings and gloves.

Vegetable fibres

The majority are 'bast' fibres, the material being extracted from the inner bark of the stem; otherwise the fibre is recovered in four cases from the leaves and in two each from the seed-coverings and from the roots. Currently the industrial world uses about 45% cotton, 16% jute, 7% wool, 4% hemp, 2½% flax, a small amount of silk — and 25% man-made fibres.

Flax (fig.15c) is the only vegetable fibre which is both native, probably, and has been grown in quantity in Europe. The species most commonly planted, *Linum usitatissimum,* is not known wild; *Linum angustifolium,* used for nets and cords by the lake communities of Neolithic Switzerland, is a native of the Mediterranean. Until affected by mechanised cotton about 1800, flax was grown by small farmers all over

Europe, the family preparing, spinning and using it them-selves too, for shirts, sheets and other 'linen'. From about 1830, the trade being mechanised then, those who still planted flax sold their crops to industry. Cultivation has continued to contract, so that most European flax, 15% of the world's commercial crop, is now grown in the small zone of northern France, Belgium and Holland; the other 85% is produced in East Europe and Russia. Ireland has the greatest output of linen cloth in Europe. The high price of flax at the time of writing may lead to increased planting.

Three other small indigenous plants have been used by Europeans. Nettle fibre was extracted in West Europe up to the last century. The common mallow's fibre has been spun and woven into cloth since Rome's classical period; about 600 AD, Isidore of Seville described a cloth called *melocinea* 'made of the thread of mallows'; from the time of Charlemagne there is the line 'Wrapt in a mallow shawl the lady shines'; and the cloth was made into the last century in Spain. Fibre mallows are grown up to 56°N in west Siberia. The use of Spanish broom, native to south Spain and North Africa, ranges from Pliny's mention of it at Cartagena, in south-east Spain, for 'mattresses, shoes and coarse garments' to its use into this century right around the Mediterranean. There is room both for research — the re-identification of the 'bulb' which yielded a fibre from which the ancient Greeks made socks, for example — and for experiments with European plants.

Four European trees have yielded fibres, the elm, lime, fir and spruce. Fibre from Norway spruce roots has been used in north Scandinavia for sewing together the thin fir planks of light portable boats, that from white spruce roots by the Canadian Indians for stitching the birch-bark exteriors onto their canoes.

Four bast fibres are imported in quantity from the east. Only hemp, a native of temperate Asia, is grown in Europe; it was a well-known crop in England over a millenium ago. Its successful cultivation in America dates from its arrival in 1629 at Plymouth. Abaca, called 'manilla hemp', is a good fibre in its own right. Botanically of the nettle family, ramie gives a high-quality fibre; it reached Europe in 1810 but, like the other basts, was slow to be mechanised. Industrialisation brought jute to Europe, notably to the Dundee mills, but in India it has an immemorial use in domestic textiles: cords, sacks, net-bags for bullock loads, a swinging cradle, a hanging pot-shelf, floorcloths, waist and hair bands, actors' wigs, cattle-muzzles . . .

It is possible that a fibre recently reported by archaeologists as 'cactus', used for a Peruvian mummy shroud of the pre-cotton period, was in fact extracted from a species of agave; this would make a sisal the earliest spun fibre in America. The author has given a detailed description of an experimental sisal plantation and extraction industry in a recent book on the island of Fuerteventura, one of the Canaries. In Central America the yucca *Yucca filamentosa* plays the part of the sisal: the 20 ft. stem is known as 'Adam's needle' and the fibre-bearing fronds as 'Eve's thread.'

Mineral fibres

Gold was hand-spun in Britain as early as the Iron Age, for it had been used as yarn in a cloth found in the tomb of a Belgic chief. The Romans spun it too: a burial discovered in Rome itself, in 1544, included a garment and a pall holding 36 lbs of gold. A Roman matron making robes for her two sons on their elevation to the Consulship is contemporarily described:

'Her well-train'd thumb protracts the length'ning gold
And makes the metal to the threads adhere.'

Silver has been used to great effect, as when King Herod Agrippa of Judaea, in a tunic 'all made of silver, and wonderful in its texture', appeared at dawn in the theatre 'and the silver, in the first sun, glittered as to terrify the beholders, so that his flatterers began to call aloud, saluting him as a god.' Imitations of the cloth, equally successful in effect, have recently appeared in the world of pop music.

Amianthine fabric was first made, perhaps, for the shrouds of classical times, so that on the funeral pyre the ashes of different bodies would remain separate. It was woven from spun asbestos and flax. A Milanese noble of the Middle Ages, interested in fire-fighting, had a complete asbestos suit, whilst Charlemagne used to throw his asbestos table-cloth in the fire after a meal to amaze his guests. Asbestos-bearing rocks occur throughout the world.

Recently-invented fibres

Natural materials used in recent years have included 'protein' fibres, such as casein, ground-nuts, maize, soya beans and eggs. Chicken feathers have been tried. Non-precious metals, glass and paper have been spun for different purposes. In all cases the spinning has of course been done by machine.

Hooke, seeing the silkworm at work, suggested in 1664 'an artificial glutinous composition' which would be drawn out 'into small wires for use'. Two centuries later Chardonnet patented a process in which cellulose, impregnated with nitrate, was placed in a solution of alcohol and ether — this artificial glutinous composition was then squirted through fine holes to solidify in the air. Now a quarter of the world's industrial output of yarn consists of man-made fibre.

CHAPTER 5

SHEEP AND THEIR FLEECES

The fleece of an average sheep easily provides a person's wool clothing for the year. A sheep is an undemanding animal and — when a dog is not used on it — unafraid of man. It thrives best on individual attention, as in pre-industrial Europe. The shearing of a trusting sheep is painless for it; its fleece, nowadays unnaturally heavy, would anyway drop off of its own accord sooner or later. The man—sheep relationship can be symbiotic rather than exploitative.

The evolution of the sheep

There are still wild sheep — all short-coated and mountain-dwellers — most species being in Asia, a few in south Europe, North Africa and North America. One of the least-known, *Ammotragus lervia,* has recently been described by the author in a work on the western Sahara. The first domesticated sheep (Chapter 2) were descended from the mouflon *(Ovis musimon, O. orientalis)*, the urial *(O. vignei)*, and the argali *(O. ammon)*, wild in the Middle East, their range including all that of the bezoar goat; the mouflon also lived in several large Mediterranean islands, perhaps just surviving there still.

Britain's Neolithic sheep came from the continent, probably in the fourth millenium BC; they may have been of urial origin and small and brown. The European Bronze Age sheep are thought to have been urial-mouflon descendants. Sheep bones increase in frequency at British sites of the last millenia BC: rare in the Neolithic, 16% of animal remains by the late Bronze Age, 88% at Iron Age Glastonbury. Prehistoric information is sketchy.

The wool exported from Britain in the sixth century BC came from small sheep with black faces. They had the two coats already described, short-fine and long-coarse. In seeking long, fine fleeces, breeding has aimed at increasing the inner coat at the expense of the outer, so that many types have lost this or at least have much finer exterior coats. Breeding has also aimed at white sheep, the colour of the more evolved species introduced by the Romans; sheep bones average 40% at Roman sites in Britain. To protect their sheep's comparatively-fine fleeces from the burrs of the South Downs, the animals were pastured in skin jackets.

The less sophisticated native sheep, their wool used for the fourth-century capes and rugs made for export, have closely-similar descendants in the sheep of the remote isles of Soay, one of the St. Kilda group, and of Cardigan. The present Soays have 1-1½ lb fleeces, mainly dark brown but ranging to fawn; the inner fibres have a diameter of 15-25 mc (a micron is a millionth of a metre), the outer of 30-50 mc. Table 4 gives comparable characteristics for the main modern British breeds' fleeces.

Another primitive British breed, the Hebridean, is extinct in the islands but may be the ancestor of the four-horned St. Kilda and Jacob's sheep, the former still alive in parks and zoos and the latter now increasingly bred commercially. Two more ancient types, believed related, are the Manx Loghtan and the Orkney, the latter now only found on North Ronaldsay, there living mainly off seaweed. The Cladagh breed of western Ireland — in Connemara and the Aran Islands — has also been compared to the Orkney sheep. The Shetlands have two peculiar strains: the Moorit, said to be closest to the Soay, and the Improved, perhaps nearest to the Orkney. There is thought to be a Norse-imported element running through some of these breeds, otherwise presumably descended from the prehistoric British sheep, like the Soay. There is by no means agreement on the intricacies of these ancient breeds; the subject is extensively discussed in Ryder's many publications.

At some stage of the Roman to Medieval span of time, the imported white and the native British sheep were crossed. This gave a breed which survived in the Highlands until about 1850. Known as the Dunface or Scottish Shortwool, it was described as 22 inches high at the shoulder, thin and lank in shape, with short erect horns, face and legs white, very short tail, the variably-coloured wool very fine; with its fibres only 3 inches long, a fleece weighed a pound. These sheep were also milked. The tiny Dunface had names and lived with the family, being taken indoors at night.

The current period of European breeding history begins with records of the merino sheep in Moorish Spain of the late Middle Ages — the time of the appearance of the spinning wheel in Europe and of the first developments in its textile trade. Export from Spain of the fine-woolled animals themselves — the admiration of Europe — was not allowed until 1765. The merino went to Germany and as the 'Saxony' breed then spread widely, to become the world's finest sheep.

In Britain of the late Middle Ages, sheep-rearing interacted with tillage in the evolution of agriculture. Three breed-groups developed:
(a)   those grazing and fertilising the fallow fields of the southern crop-lands, such as the short-wool Down sheep
(b)   those with their own non-arable pastures, for example the Marsh and Fen long-wool breeds
(c)   those with their own rough grazing, such as the English, Welsh and Scottish hill sheep.

In Scotland, change did not bring great variety. About the fourteenth century an improved white sheep, the Cheviot, spread from northern England into the Lowlands, gradually replacing its relative the Dunface. In the Highlands however, the ancient breed continued as described until

1750—1850. Then the new land-owning class, seeking money by supplying wool to the now-mechanising textile industry, had them 'cleared', often with their owners, to make way for the argali-type Blackface.

Britain's most valued breeds, second only to the merinos — the climate is too wet for these — have been widely exported over the last centuries and have greatly influenced the world's stock. European colonisation and industrialisation, each starting about 1500, diffused the sheep to Central and South America from sixteenth-century Spain, then to North America in 1609, to South Africa in 1785 and to New Zealand and Australia about 1788, these last four regions getting their animals from Britain.

The world's sheep breeds now roughly divide into 40% merino, 20% crosses, 40% other breeds; interbreeding is done to increase wool, meat and resistance to local conditions. The domestic sheep's present distribution is shown in fig. 5; world production of raw wool in 1974—5 was about 2600 million kilos, contributed as indicated. Britain's output has increased by a million tons a year in the nineteen seventies so that it now stands at 51 million kilos; however, 44 million kilos was already being produced in 1800.

Half the world's wool is grown in the European colonies of the southern hemisphere for the industrial states of the northern hemisphere. Consumption of this fresh wool now averages USSR, East Europe, China 35%, Japan 10%, UK 10%, France 9%, Italy 7%, USA 4%, West Germany 3%, Australia 2%, Belgium 2%, other countries 18%.

The characteristics of wool

The qualities of a spun yarn — strength, elasticity, resilience, warmth, dye-absorption — depend primarily upon its component fibres. In cross-section a sheep-wool fibre consists of a central core, or medulla, surrounded by a ring of cortex which is, in turn, encased in the outer, scaly cuticle. The visible edges of the scales, or imbrications (fig.2, human, but similar to coarse sheep-wool), lie towards the outer tip of the fibre; the wool's binding quality, and thus its strength, increases with the number of imbrications, a fine merino having up to 2800 surfacing an inch's length of a single hair, against the 600 imbrications of an inch of Blackface wool. Each fibre tapers towards the outer tip. Strength also increases with width and length. The diameter of sheep-wool fibres, often elliptical rather than round, is usually 15—45 mc, limits 10—90 mc; a sheep's fleeces grow coarser with age. Fibre length varies from an inch in the Soay and only half an inch more in the shorter Down breeds to the 16 inches of the Lincoln fleece; merinos have only 2 inch fibres. An undernourished or unhealthy sheep will produce a weak fibre.

Elasticity and resilience increase with the waviness of the fibres, for this allows temporary distortion without permanent re-shaping; the same characteristic partially determines the air-spaces in a spun yarn, the warmth increasing proportionately. Waviness rises with imbrication count. This 'crimp' is usually judged by eye rather than measured. Finally, dye-absorption depends on the chemical composition of the fibre. The greater the proportion of primitive-stage, outer-coat hairs, the more uneven will be the result, since these 'kemps' resist the dye. Over-absorption can occur, for example by the rotted tips of a wet-mountain sheep's fleece.

From the view-point of a machine, uniformity is a further desirable quality. Hand-spinning is more adaptable.

No sheep produces wool of optimum type under all these headings. The value of a wool depends upon its combination of qualities.

However, a further factor is the use to which the yarn will be put. The long-standing divisions are into woollen and, increasingly since the seventeenth century, worsted. Put simply, woollens are dense, felted, springy cloths; short wools are used. Worsteds are lighter and smooth-surfaced, the fibres parallel; into these go the long, lustrous wools.

A wool classification commonly met is by each type's

capacity to be spun finely; standardisation began in the proto-industrial eighteenth century, using the check reel (Chapter 9). This classification is a guide to some qualities but not, of course, to others. About twenty fibres are the minimum, in cross-section, which will hold together to form a yarn. The index (table 4) shows that, for example, a pound of Southdown wool can be spun at the most into 60 skeins of a standard 560 yards each, the British maximum. The wool-counts traditionally used are 90, 80, 70, 64, 60, 58, 56, 54, 52, 50, 48, 46, 44, 36, 32, 28 skeins; the preparation of the raw wool is as for worsted yarn (Chapter 6).

Internationally, 60 and above is called 'merino', a synonym for high quality, whilst 44 and below puts a wool into the 'carpet' category.

British breeds and their fleeces

Table 4 gives details of the sheep most commonly found in the UK. There is considerable variation both within each breed and within an individual fleece — thus a breed will have a range of uses. The 'group' column refers to spinning capacity (fine, average, coarse), length of fibre (short, medium, long) and habitat (plains, hills). Crimp is highest in the Downs sheep, middling in the other low-ground breeds, least in the hill-sheep. The many rarer breeds (England and Wales 13.7%, Scotland 5.7%, Ireland 5%, UK 14.3%) include the increasingly-popular four-horned Jacob's sheep, giving a 4—6 lb black-and-white fleece, 44s—56s in texture and 3—6 inches in fibre-length; its British Wool Marketing Board price in August 1977 was £4.15 a fleece.

The balance of the table is composed of the important cross-bred sheep: England and Wales 24%, Scotland 21%, Ireland 34%, UK 23%. The main types are the Blackface—Border Leicester, for carpets, and the Blackface—Cheviot for furnishing fabrics.

Table 4: Main Breeds of British Sheep

Main British breeds	Spinning limit	Fibre length (ins.)	Fibre weight (lbs)	Fleece colour	Group	Use (fine to coarse)	BWMB Fleece price Aug.'77	1974 wool production (%) England & Wales	Scotland	Ireland	UK total
Southdown Dorset Down, Horn	50-60	1½-3½	4-6½	White	FSP	Fine clothing, blankets	£7.40	.6	0	0	.4
Shetland	56-58	1-4	1½-2½	White, brown, grey black	FSH	Shawls, scarves, knitwear	£2.70	0	.1	0	.1
Suffolk Down Suffolk Cross	56-58	2½	5	White	FSP	Fine clothing, blankets	£7.40	.3	4	3	1
Shropshire Clun, Kerry	50-58	4	6	White	FSP	ditto	£5.65	16	.4	0	12
Radnor & Cross	50-58	4½	4½		FSH			11	0	0	7
Cheviot	50-56	4	4¾	White, grey, black	FSH	Fine clothing, tweed, carpets	£6.60	.7	18	4	5
Welsh Mountain	50-56	3	2¾	Grey, black	FSH	Knitting yarn, flannel, blankets, tweeds	£1.90	12	.1	0	8
Exmoor Horn	48-56	3½	6½		FSH			.8	0	0	.6

Main British breeds	Spinning limit	Fibre length (ins.)	Fibre weight (lbs)	Fleece colour	Group	Use (fine to coarse)	BWMB Fleece price Aug.'77	1974 wool production (%)			
								England & Wales	Scotland	Ireland	UK total
Derbyshire Gritstone, Lonk	36-50	5-7	5		AMH			1	0	0	.7
Kent or Romney Marsh	44-48	7½	8½	White	AMP	Knitting yarn, tweeds, coats	£8.60	4	0	0	3
Border Leicester, Leicester	40-48	6-12	7½-11½	White	AMP ALP	Worsteds furnishing fabrics	£7.75	.1	.6	1	.3
Lincoln	36-44	13	13½	Lustrous white	CLP	Worsteds, carpets		.3	0	0	.2
Swaledale	32-40	8	3½		CLH	Knitting yarn, tweed, carpets		7	.1	0	5
Herdwick	28-40	10	3½	White, grey, black	CLH	Blankets, carpets	£2.60	.5	0	0	.4
Blackface	28-40	10	4½	White, brown, grey, black	CLH	Tweeds, carpets		3	50	53	16
Devon Longwool	32-36	10	13		CLP			5	0	0	3

65

Obtaining wool in modern Britain

Until recently, British wool-workers acquired their material
in three different ways. The larger manufacturers had con-
tracts direct with the big farmers. The smaller clothiers
bought from the staplers, wholesalers who originally
travelled around the farms buying wool. The craftsman also
bought direct from the farmers, doing so privately or in the
market-place. A wool 'pack' weighed 240 pounds. The poor,
needing wool to make their own clothes, either gleaned it
off the fields and hedges or, as in the Welsh *gwlana* custom,
right after shearing went on a week's wool-begging circuit
of the area's farms.

The sale of wool is now controlled by the British Wool
Marketing Board, begun in 1950. Owners of more than four
sheep must register with the Board and, if wishing to sell the
wool, can only do so to the Board. The procedure is for the
owner to send his summer's wool to a merchant of his choice
(Appendix 4); the merchant grades it, packs it and receives a
commission from the Board. About 70% of the wool
reaches the Board's forty merchants between July and
September. The government and the Board work out a price
for each of the 700 grades (350 greasy, 350 washed) and
from this deduct the forecast costs of marketing, including
commissions and transport, to arrive at the rates to be paid
to the sheep-owners.

Next the Committee of London Wool Brokers auctions
the wool, doing so at two dozen auctions, spread throughout
the twelve subsequent months, in Bradford, Exeter and
Edinburgh. Between 2½—4 million pounds are sold at each
auction; sample bales of each lot are on view. The proceeds
are sent to the Board; surpluses and small deficits are
written off to the State.

The spinner, then, is not allowed to buy wool from a
neighbouring farmer, a current example of industrial
centralisation at the expense of human society. Instead, the
fleeces have to be handled by merchants, auctioneers, the
Board, the wholesaler and the retailer. The average price paid
to the sheep owners for the 1974—5 shearing was 26 pence

a pound, less 3.9 pence marketing, 22.1 pence nett. The cheapest way for the spinner to buy wool is to do so *personally* from the Board's depots, listed in Appendix 4; the prices for whole fleeces, these varying greatly in quality and weight, are given in table 4. The rates can vary with recent auction prices, these changing with supply and demand in the textile industry. The Board will also supply by post at the figures shown in the table; postage is then a further expense to the spinner, although the Board keeps this low, presumably to allow for the amount already deducted, for marketing, from the price paid to the sheep-owner.

Now it can be calculated that the *lowest* price for a pound of wool from the Board is over twice the *average* price paid to the sheep-owners. And of course the normal retailers ask more still. Between these come the two hundred British merchants but, other than those acting as Board depots, most will not sell small quantities of wool.

Absurdly, another government agency will be found trying simultaneously to artificially stimulate the textile crafts, in particular by the grants system. However, only formalised profit-oriented workshops will be approved for this aid by the civil servants concerned, a further example of centralised control. At best, the commercial craftsman gets a compensatory subsidy with its implication that his work is in an artificial category; at worst, the family and community craftsman supports a chain of businessmen and civil servants through greatly-inflated prices.

Textile craftsmen should work to become exceptions to this system, designed to benefit industry. Farmers in the Outer Hebrides can sell their fleeces direct to the local spinning mills — there are effectively no hand-spinners left — to help the survival of Britain's internationally-prestigious tweed industry. This exemption could be extended to small wool-workers all over Britain, defined if needs be by a yearly maximum consumption of fleeces. Further choices are to continue to persuade farmers to sell fleeces direct anyway — not all that difficult, since many see the absurdity of the system — or to rear the sheep oneself.

The British wool industry, 1975

There are about 90,000 registered sheep owners, 49% in England, 20% in Wales, 20% in Scotland, 11% in Northern Ireland. Between them they have 3% of the world's sheep or 30,000,000 animals, an average 300—350 animals each; the total may be compared to the figure two centuries ago, 1774, about 10,000,000 sheep. The 1975 flocks gave 112,000,000 lb of wool, almost 4 lb a sheep. Of this total, 35,000,000 lb came from slaughtered carcasses, the other two-thirds from shorn animals; this 77,000,000 lb stemmed 71% from England and Wales, 25% from Scotland, 4% from Northern Ireland. Though the owners are going down in number, the sheep and their wool are increasing.

Exports of British wool totalled 35,000,000lb (£17,000,000) mainly of the coarsest fleeces. In particular, Blackface is sent to Italy for mattress-stuffing (£5,000,000). Germany and the USA were also buyers.

Against the 77,000,000lb of British wool left in Britain, the trade consumed about 240,000,000lb, the balance being imported. The wool used represented 48% of the 500,000,000lb of varied fibres required by industry. Trends for the nineteen-seventies are that overall fibre consumption is dropping, as is that of wool, but the use of artificial fibres is increasing (38% in 1975).

The spinning counts of the wool used were: 60 and over, 65,000,000lb; 50—58, 61,000,000lb; 46—50, 57,000,000lb; below 44, 44,000,000lb; unspecified, 13,000,000lb. Each trends down, the coarsest the least, in the nineteen seventies.

The type of spinning, fully explained in the next chapter, is best shown by a table:

	Total	Wool	Artificial	Other
Woollen spinning and felts	287	142	89	56
Worsted spinning	213	98	101	14
Total (million lb)	500	240	190	70

Finally, three products of interest to the textile craftsman:

	Total	Worsted	Semi-worsted	Woollen
All yarns (million lb)	414	148	20	246
Carpet & rug yarns (million lb)	132	2	11	119
Woven fabrics (million sq yd)	181	89	----	92

All these figures trend downwards too. Hand-spinning and
weaving, happily not subject to rigid statistical control, are
probably increasing.

CHAPTER 6

THE PREPARATION OF WOOL FOR HAND—SPINNING

The modern spinner has to decide how far the following complex techniques are necessary, bearing in mind the state of the wool-craft at the time of its evolutionary peak, the eighteenth century. The craftsmen were under extreme pressure. First, as employees in the primitive factories:

> *'As first, the Parter, that doth neatly cull*
> *The finer from the coarse sort of wool.*
> *The Dyer then in order next doth stand,*
> *With sweating brow and a laborious hand.*
> *With oil they then asperge it, which being done,*
> *The careful hand of mixers round it run,*
> *The Stock-carder his arms doth hard employ*
> *(Remembering Friday is our Market day).*
> *Then Knee-carder doth (without control)*
> *Quickly convert it to a lesser roll*
> *Which done, the Spinster doth in hand it take,*
> *And of two hundred rolls one thread doth make.'*

Subsequently the craftsmen had to compete with the machines.

However, there seems no reason for the modern craftsman to imitate the machines' uniformity, something of an end in itself at present. So the spinner can choose, adapt and invent processes according to the desired yarn. Carding, for example, was absolutely essential once the hand-turned wheel was introduced, since it was impossible to tease out and feed in unprepared wool rapidly so long as one hand had to break off frequently to turn the wheel; yet the invention of the flyer-treadle wheel was simply balanced by an increased output and sophistication of the yarns and cloths — instead of saving labour, it increased profit — so that carding continued. In fact, all depends on the fleece and the use of the yarn. For heavy yarns, for example, the author spins straight from a Blackface fleece with no preparation.

Separating the wool from the sheep

Since wild sheep regularly moult in the summer, the early domestic breeds probably had their short coats plucked off them just before, as is still done with the last British primitive breeds. As the sheep evolved and cutting became necessary, this may have been done in the Middle East with flint-bladed knives, used also for grain-harvesting and other work; when advanced sheep were taken to St. Kilda in the nineteenth century, the islanders cut the wool off with iron knives. Around 9000 years after the taming of the first sheep, iron was smelted and shears were made.

Sheep are usually clipped or shorn in the summer after their birth. The shepherd still sometimes gives them a wash first. They are then closely penned together so that, warmed, the grease in the wool makes the fleece supple to the handler. The shearer takes the wool off in one piece, recognisably sheep-shaped, as this helps the sorter. In New Zealand a team of nine sheared 3156 sheep in nine hours, 39 each an hour. Taking a fleece off a sheep can, however, be a vivid experience.

A third of the wool in Britain comes from slaughtered sheep. A chemical process is used, resulting in the skin releasing the fibres. This wool, poorer than that from the live sheep, is used for coarse fabrics such as blankets and carpets.

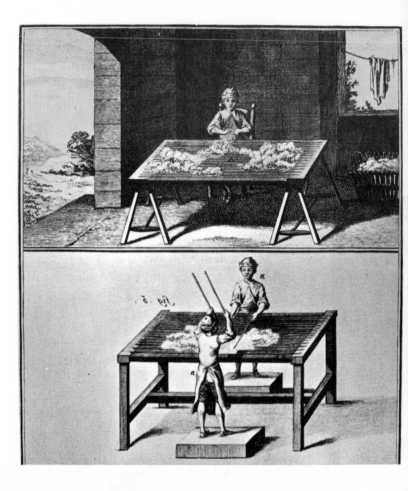

16. Boys sorting and beating wool, France, 1750

Sorting the wool

This process divides up the fleece into pieces, the different types of wool going into different yarns. The sorter works on a slatted or netting-covered table, so that burrs, dirt and so on fall through. Fig.16 shows a boy at work in a spacious well-ventilated rural workshop about 1750.

Alternatively, the visitors to Winchcombe's sixteenth-century factory described how:

> 'To another room came they
> Where children were in poor array;
> And everyone sate picking wool,
> The finest from the coarse to cull...'

The finest wool, 1 (fig.15a), is along the shoulders; 2 is irregular, often with burrs; 3 is shorter and coarser; 4 more so; 5, 6, short, worn, dirty; 7 short, stiff, straight. The sorter divides the fleece down the middle, then tears the halves into qualities; the looser impurities are removed. Rough blending may also be done at this stage: heaps are made of each quality, piece on piece, and then strips are torn off the edge of each piece, working down the heap's side: each new smaller pile then goes as a batch to the next process.

The eighteenth-century sequence, from this point, was usually cleaning-dyeing-blending-oiling-carding or combing-spinning. The modern spinner, often not dyeing, will best card or comb first, if necessary, then spin and finally wash the wool. The full ancient sequence will be followed through in the next sections.

Cleaning the wool

A coarse British fleece, when just shorn, averages 69% fibre, 12% earth and sand, 8% water, 7% suint (sweat), 3% grease, 1% vegetable matter. Most breeds' fleeces lose between 35–50% on cleaning, the merino averaging 45% loss; in very hot climates there can be 30% dirt and 40% suint, leaving only 30% wool.

There has been some use of the vibrating bow (fig.18 bcd) for wool cleaning in Europe, possibly dating from the pre-historic period. This will be best described in the section on cotton preparation.

Generally, wool is washed to clean it. Preferably it is soaked beforehand. The water should be soft, rain water if possible, to save soap and avoid a lime deposit on the fibres; this makes the wool feel rough and would cause uneven dyeing.

Three parts of water, not too hot, were used to one part of urine; this was collected from house to house in Europe into the last century. An excess of alkali should also be avoided. The suint is itself a natural soap, 'lanolin', a mixture of potash salts and oil, soluble in cold water.

There are many alternatives to urine. Plant roots such as those of the soapwort, *Saponaria oficinalis,* were used in ancient Italy and Greece, yucca roots by the Mexican peasants. The most common scouring agent was plant ash. Land plants burned for this have been saltworts and glassworts, seaweeds have been of many species. In Europe generally, this crude soda was called 'barilla'. In Highland Britain, bracken and the seaweed *Ascophyllum nodosum* were, respectively, the main land and marine plants.

Between 1730—1830, the developing textile industry, in need of immense quantities of scouring agent, took over the simple rural craft. In Highland Scotland, for example, the peasantry who made 'kelp' from the seaweed were exploited — with the highly-profitable participation of the owners of their small patches of land — to a degree rarely surpassed anywhere. As well as keeping 80% or so of the kelp's selling price, the landowners put rents up and up . . . when industry suddenly went over to the Le Blanc process — the extraction of soda from salt — its distant slaves could not pay these new rents. The landowners, now used to the increased income, then decided that sheep and deer were more profitable and 'cleared' the poverty-stricken peasants, many having to emigrate. The author has described the south Hebridean kelp-makers and the Canary Island barilla industry in other books.

The craftsman has nowadays to rid the commercial fleece of the various chemical dips in which the sheep has been immersed to combat its parasites; dipping is not obligatory at present. Probably it was worse when tar and butter were

17. Washing, rinsing and drying wool, France, 1750

smeared on instead — as much as a gallon of the first and 10 lbs of the second to twenty sheep. The modern coloured marking fluids, replacing red ruddle, are hard to remove; industry does so by a chemical process.

If rinsed in a river (fig.17), the wool is best in baskets, especially if short-fibred. For wringing out, two long poles with twisting hooks on the ends can be used, most easily with long-fibred wool; a mangle is also useful. Dyeing is most effectively done at this stage, as opposed to once the wool is spun; this craft merits a book to itself. The wool can be dried on racks, as illustrated.

Beating the wool

This was known as 'willowing' or 'willeying' since willow sticks were used. The beating was done on a strong frame

75

known as a 'felking board', to open and get rid of the dust (this last not shown in fig.16). The children — drawn with huge arms but small bodies — were replaced from 1733 by a machine designed by Kay, inventor of the flying shuttle. The beating was done by spring-loaded laths raised by tappets mounted on a wheel.

Felt, woollen or worsted

From this stage the treatment of the wool follows one of three courses. For felt the wool is simply matted into a sheet, as will be described, without spinning; using up the shortest wool, except where felt is more important than spun yarn, the fibres are deliberately prepared so that they lie in all directions. A woven 'cloth', in medieval terminology, or 'woollen', is made of spun, high-imbrication wavy fibres which have been prepared as for felt; it is later made more solid by wetting and pummelling — 'milling', or 'waulking' in the Hebrides — to increase its felt-like characteristics. A 'stuff' or 'worsted' is however woven from yarn spun from long lustrous wool in which the fibres have first been aligned. A Harris tweed is a typical woollen, a camel-hair coat an ordinary worsted. A 'serge' is a cloth woven with a worsted warp and a woollen weft. The spinner must also take into account whether the yarn is to be a warp or a weft, the former needing long-fibred wool. There have been infinite variations and combinations in making yarns. The basic distinction between woollens and worsteds was already made in Aristophanes' time, the fifth century BC, whilst the Romans had togas of each type.

'May your wands be like sinews'

The Mongolians turn all their wool into felt. Using an iron tool shaped like a thumbless hand, they comb the inner coats off their sheep in the spring, clip off the outer coat in the autumn. Since long as well as short wool is used, the felt is very strong.

The wool is first fluffed up with rods, the workers singing as they beat. A layer of this wool, several inches deep, is then spread on a grass or reed mat, this next rolled up extremely tightly. It is then pushed to and fro between two lines of singing workers and, finally, dragged around the plain by a galloping horse. If, for example, a family needs to renew its tent, it announces a felt-making day: the neighbours come and take full part in the work, the family providing a feast. The passing traveller should shout 'May your wands be like sinews!' In Central Asia the craft's antiquity is probably as great as that of spinning and weaving in the Middle East.

The primitive European felt industry was more complicated. The wool was carded, a technique described shortly, to allow very fine layers, or 'laps', to be prepared. These were then subjected to simultaneous moisture, heat, pressure and rubbing by passage through a mangle-like implement which, partially immersed in a trough of water, had a heavy, oscillating upper roller and a hollow, steam-heated lower roller. Layer was added to layer, the first and last being the best wool.

In addition to sheep's wool, various other animal fibres have gone into felts: rabbit and hare, otter, coypu, beaver and musquash, vicuña, cow. The 'hatte of biever' has been worn by 'the nobels of the lande' since at least the twelfth century. It is noteworthy that this amazingly delicate and technical craft, only slowly mechanised, used a bow (fig.18c) to prepare the wool (see Chapter 7, final section, for technique); the bow was seven feet long with a catgut cord which was vibrated by a wooden tool like a double-ended sewing mushroom (b). The felting properties of the wool, usually beaver on the outside and rabbit on the inside, were greatly increased by 'carroting', treatment with a solution of nitrate of mercury. As a modern household craft, felting seems little explored, yet it is suggestive that using wooden moulds, the Swedes made felt socks until not long ago.

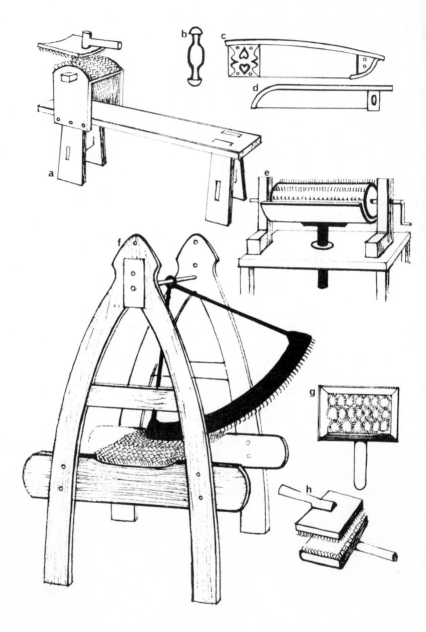

18. *Fibre preparation: Swedish carding bench (a), wool bow and vibrator,*
beaver hat trade (bc), prehistoric fibre bow, Europe (d), Paul's 1748
carder (e), Corsican swinging carder (f), teazle card (g), hand cards (h)

78

Carding the wool

The aim of carding is to loosen, mix and lubricate the fibres; more impurities will drop out. Carding, by increasing the air-spaces amongst the fibres, makes a warmer yarn.

For two millenia and probably longer, carding depended upon the teazle (fig.15e), *Dipsacus fullonum,* a tall thistle; this can be found in Britain on roadsides and rough ground, being increasingly common southwards. Selected teazle heads were set in a handled wooden frame, square or rectangular (fig.18g); this was called a 'card', from the Latin *carduus,* thistle. The flexible bristles making up the head are each tipped with a minute hook, these seizing the wool fibres and 'teazling' them out, as will be described. Since Iron Age Glastonbury used frames set with thorns — as had the Neolithic Swiss lake-people — it may well be that the Romans introduced the *carduus* type. Teazles, in triangular frames, were used for raising the nap on woven cloth; better than metal teeth, they are still part of nap-raising *machines.*

Metal-toothed cards are first recorded in the thirteenth century AD; the quantity of techniques first appearing in records about this time may be as much due to the crafts being poorly reported before this as to the accelerating evolution of the medieval wool-trade. Still, as has been said, the new hand-wheel could not be used without carding the wool well first. The new finer-toothed cards (fig.18h) produced a more slender, longer yarn from the same amount of wool. Late in the seventeenth century the carding bench (fig.18a) and 'stock' cards were in use. One card was usually fixed to the bench, as drawn; those benches in the early factories had a high desk-like front, the card surface, on top, sloping down towards the worker. At its most advanced the other card hung from the ceiling against a counter-weight, the cord from this stock-card running through a pulley. Stock-cards were larger than the ordinary 'knee-cards'; the hanging card often had a second handle sticking up from the middle of its back, to allow more strength to be used. This system doubled the output of prepared wool. The knee-cards continued to be used by the children in the factories.

Card-making, for long a small craft, was in turn industrialised once the factory system got under way. The manufacturers handed out the metal teeth by weight to the peasantry, these turned in the finished cards. The last chapter contains a detailed description of how these cards were made.

The basic actions of carding, like those of any craft technique, are quickly acquired. If the wool has been washed and dyed, it is now best oiled. Melted goose-grease, sheep tallow or pig fat were used; olive oil was an alternative, 3—4 oz to a pound of weft, 1½—2 oz to a pound of warp, for fine spinning. A cheap cooking oil could be used nowadays.

A thin layer of oil-sprinkled wool, the worst parts teased out by the hands already, is spread on the teeth of one card; this faces upwards, held by the left hand, handle away from the body, back resting on the left knee (fig.l). The other card, empty, facing downwards, handle towards the body, is drawn across the first and towards the body. This action is repeated a few times and then the two cards are reversed. Eventually the wool is evenly spread and aligned on the two cards; it will be well embedded. More wool is then added on top and this is carded into the first layers. When the teeth are· full, the wool is freed by hooking the front edge-teeth of one card into the front edge of the wool on the other, peeling back the layer. The wool can be left in flat rectangles or made into rolls such as can be seen by the spinner's right foot in Millet's drawing. These cardings are now ready for hand-spinning. The Highland Scots kept their *rolagan* in a special container, the *mudag;* unaccountably oval, like a rugby ball, it had a hole in the centre of its side for the passage of the wool.

Blending can be done at this stage too, the different fibres being carded into each other. This may be a mixing of wool with wool or with cotton, silk and other fibres, either to get specific yarns or for adulteration. Colours, natural and dyed, are also blended, for example in tweed yarns.

Carding was comparatively easy to mechanise. Paul's mangle-like machine of 1748 (fig.18e) used a roller bearing strips of toothed cloth; the concave face of the plate below

80

was also covered with carding fabric; to remove the carded wool, the under-plate was lowered and a fine-toothed comb, the 'needlestick', the length of the roller, used to peel it off. Arkwright's version of 1775 (fig.13), in the second stage of textile-machinery inventions, was the forerunner of the massive carders of the next century. However, for fifty years the machines produced only short lengths, hence the child 'pieceners', already described.

But the spinning machines could not digest the pieced-together fleecy rolls. These were thus next combined, up to six at a time, to make a more even 'sliver'. This was then passed through a pre-spinning 'drawing frame' (fig.22e). This had two pairs of rollers, the second pair turning at 3.4 times the first, a principle best fully explained in Chapter 9, on spinning, since it is in fact simply an adaptation — by Arkwright — of Paul's 1738 spinning-machine design (fig. 22d). The drawing frame stretched out the wool and gave it a slight twist, a process usually repeated twice more. This thinner, coherent wool was now called a 'slubbing'; the thinnest, most twisted slubbings, like coarse loose yarns, were known as 'rovings'.

The modern craftsman wanting to build a carder more advanced than the knee and bench-stock types, yet still use human energy and judgement, might try adapting Paul's design or could consider the swinging carder used in Corsica (fig.18f). The following principles should be borne in mind: one or both toothed surfaces can move; they can move in different directions or in the same direction at different speeds; one set of teeth caused to move points foremost will strip the wool off the other set. The design of the teeth is important: they have always been elastic and bent at 135° so that, in continual collision with those of the opposing card, they both yield and fall back towards their mounting cloth, thus avoiding damage and allowing the carding action to continue.

Finally, there have been many sizes and settings of cards. These depended on the nature of the wool, the degree of fineness required and the use for the yarn. Each batch could pass through as many as four sets of cards, these getting finer and finer as in the table. The following specifications for cards were those prescribed by law in France early in the eighteenth century:

	Fine wools of Spain & Languedoc for first and second quality London-style woollen cloth			Ordinary Wools and cloths		
	Warp		Weft	Warp & weft		
	1st–3rd	4th	1st	1st	2nd	3rd
Size (ins)	9 x 2	9 x 2 + 2 rows	9 x 5½	9 x 5½	9 x 5½	9 x 4 + 3 rows
Rows	84	84	51	45	61	84
Teeth	43	61	60	54	61	61

Carding was so minutely regulated that the cards were to conform to the inch; the composition of the metal of the teeth was also laid down for each class. The card-maker was to brand his mark and their details on the cards. The card-user was not to use the same cards for white and dyed wools nor to card too little or too much — any breach involved confiscation of the cards and a fine. Similar processes and penalties were current throughout the primitive factories of Europe.

Combing the wool

Flax, used about as early as wool, has to be combed before it is spinnable (Chapter 7) — so combing may have originated in the linen craft. It was common in Biblical times and in Roman Britain, the combs found on the latter sites having up to 27 teeth (fig. 19f). Double-ended combs were then in use on the continent. Between that time and 1789, the craft altered little (fig. 19b) — there was no intermediate technology such as the spinning wheel or pedal loom.

Combing, used primarily on long-fibre wool, aims at alignment and the removal of all irregularities, in particular of short kempy fibres which would protrude and spoil the smoothness of the cloth. The following description is based

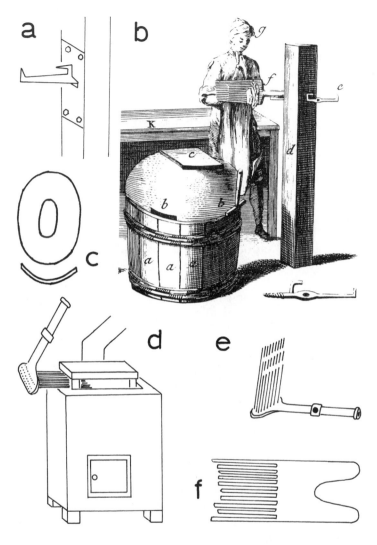

19. Fibre preparation: combing wool on a pad, with brackets (ab), diz (c), comb-heating stove (d), comb (e)

on that given in 1910 by an 82-year-old comber from Keighley in Yorkshire. Expectation of life was normally low, due to the fumes from the charcoal stoves.

The essential tools were the two combs (fig. 19e), a

stout wall bracket (ab), a holed disc of horn (c) and a heater (d). The combs, weighing 7lb each, had heads, 8 by 3 inches, embedded with long iron or steel teeth set at about 60° to the handle. There were from two to eight rows of teeth, the combs being called 'two-pitch', 'three-pitch' and so on; thirty teeth to the row may have been average; the row furthest from the handle had the longest teeth, the rows getting shorter inwards. Each tooth tapered to a sharp point. The teeth were bedded in horn, as a buffer against the shock of combing. The handle, made of ash, was 10 inches long; it had iron-lined holes about 6 inches from the end and in the very tip itself. The wall fitting, or 'pad', had two prongs which corresponded to the holes in the handle of the comb. The stove's only peculiarity was that it had to heat the combs and their embedded wool without burning them. This was achieved in Victorian Yorkshire by adding an oven-like top, not obviously efficient: the rim was raised, the comb resting on this, whilst the heat was brought on to the upper side by a stone cover raised on short legs.

The first stage, as in carding, is to replace the oil, if the wool has been washed already. Very little lubricant is needed; olive oil, rape oil and butter have each been used. The wool, usually still damp from washing, was rolled in the craftsman's oily hands. When, in the late seventeenth century, the Irish competition was under discussion, it was noted with disdain that there the spinners themselves went through 'the whole process from the sheep's back until the worsted is ready for the loom, preparing it with the worst butter . . . mixed with a mucilaginous juice got from roots'. By then industry was of course well on its way to division of labour and the conveyor belt.

The most lengthy form of process began on a preliminary pad, the 'jenny'. A heated comb was fixed on to this so that the handle was horizontal and the teeth were pointing upwards. Two ounces of fleece was then 'lashed' or 'donned' on to the comb with sweeping movements; the wool was only just snagged in the front teeth, hanging down fringe-wise towards the worker. A second comb was prepared in the same way. One comb was then attached to the pad

84

itself (fig.19b). Its teeth pointed sideways, the rows lying on their sides. The pad comb was now combed or 'jigged' with the free comb, at first engaging only the front long row of each and then gradually bringing more and more rows into play. The wool might be transferred to combs with finer, closer teeth. Care was taken that all the wool was 'straightened'. When judged finished, the wool was 'drawn off', that is pulled through the teeth so as to be thinned and elongated; it might also be drawn through the 'diz' (c), a holed oval disc of horn, concave, 2 by 1½ inches, further smoothing and regularising the fibres. The sliver, known as a 'top', might be 6 feet in length.

Any loose long fibre was added to the next batch. The unwanted short wool, accumulated around the base of the teeth, was passed to the woollen spinners; this fibre was known as 'noil'.

Shorter techniques existed. The wool might be lashed straight on to a comb already on the pad in the jigging position. Both lashing and combing might be done on the knee, as if using hand-cards, with the comb clamped on the pad only for the final drawing-off stage.

The long sliver was now ready for hand-spinning or, if a machine came next, went for drawing out into slubbings and rovings. Although the Keighley comber does not seem to have made the point, it is likely that the diz itself had — or had once had, in hand-spinning — the function of drawing out the wool too. 'Diz' seems derived from 'dizen', a word related to the Low German *diesse,* the prepared flax on the distaff, or 'dis-staff'; the origins of the horn disc might thus be found on the continent. The aperture in the Highlanders' *mudag* may have had a similar function. This use of a hole may be compared to that of the rollers in Arkwright's drawing frame (fig.22e). The hand-spinner of worsted might be able to design a tool on the diz-*mudag* principle.

Combing was the hardest of the wool-crafts to mechanise and, although Cartwright invented his machine in 1789, the combers continued in action until about 1850. This demand for their work partially accounts for their comparative freedom of spirit.

CHAPTER 7

THE PREPARATION OF VEGETABLE FIBRES

Bast fibres, yielded by the greater part of these plants, are all extracted by much the same process. This will be described for flax, together with the contrasting aspects of jute preparation. The processing of the two other main groups, leaf and seed fibres, will be illustrated by descriptions of the work involved in treating phormium and cotton.

Growing and preparing flax

The common flax-plant is a blue-flowered annual, 20—40 in tall (fig. 15c). As a crop it can be turned not only into linen yarn but into linseed oil and cattle fodder as well; these products, like lint, derive their name from the French *lin,* flax. Once grown by all European peasants, its cultivation is simple. It likes a moist subsoil, preferably a comparatively-weedless newly-tilled pasture. About three bushels of seed are sown to the acre, the stems close together to bring them up straight and tall. Weeding is essential. The crop is ready when the flowers fall or at the latest just before the capsules are ripe: they are then turning from green to brown, whilst the stalks will be two-thirds yellow in height.

The flax *must* be pulled up, preferably in dry weather.

The parallel stalks are laid out in small airy heaps, two handfuls one way and two the other. The first operation is the 'bolling' or removal of the valuable seeds, by pulling each handful through a 'ripple'; this is a fixed iron comb with rounded 18 in teeth which are 3/16" apart at their bases and, tapering from 15 in up, are ½" apart at the tips. The work can be done on a canvas sheet in the field itself. The bundles may go to the next stage at once or can be stored for the winter.

Fig. 15d shows a cross-section through a flax stalk: epidermis (1), bast fibre (2), cambium (3), woody fibres (4), pith (5). To get at the bast fibre, the outer bark must be removed. This is begun chemically, using either water or the dew to rot, or 'ret', the stalks; the bacteria destroy the gum which holds the stalk together. Water-retting, the more common, uses the waters, preferably soft, of a sunny sheltered pool or sluggish stream; iron in the water will colour the fibre. An acre's crop needs a pond or trench 50 by 9 ft; the depth should be a maximum of 4 ft, bearing in mind that 27–30°C is the optimum water temperature. The stalk bundles, tied round at each end, are packed in the pool, roots downwards. If not sunk in crates, essential in a stream, they can be weighed down with planks and stones, or by sods separated from the flax by a layer of rushes. Fermentation should begin at once, being marked by bubbles. The retting will usually take from 9–14 days, though at 30°C it is finished in four days. The state of the stalks must be regularly tested and, once the fibre separates easily from the rest, they must be removed. It might be an advantage, at this point, to wash out the loosened gum in a stream.

The bundles are now spread on a clean field for 10–14 days, with regular turning. The fibres will then be found to have partially separated themselves from the central layer, or 'shive'. Gathered up, again in dry weather, the bundles can go for fibre-extraction at once, though stooking for a period is best.

In dew-retting, the bundles, once bolled, are immediately spread on the field. They then rot under the influence of dew, rain and sunlight in 14–28 days, being regularly turned. Dew-retting has been most common in Russia, the fibre being brown.

The ancient Egyptians next beat the stalks with mallets on stone slabs, according to Pliny. In Europe this is known as 'breaking and scutching'. The main tool was like a tall bench with a heavy blunt hinged wooden arm; if mounted on the top, this came down into a shallow groove, if on the side then it just missed the edge of the bench. It was guillotine-like in aspect but designed to bend and batter and not to cut. With one hand the worker gradually pulled a bundle of stalks across the bench-top whilst, with the other, he cracked the outer bark with downward blows of the hinged arm. A mangle, with its rollers grooved, is again the alternative. Finally the bundles were threshed to get rid of the remaining core and outer bark. The bundles or 'stricks' were now made up into 14 lb bales.

A nineteenth-century experiment showed that at this point the fibre represented 9% of the harvested and air-dried stalks; these had also given about 12% seed, usually considered to be, in turn, 30% oil. British agriculture was then producing between 20—40 stones of fibre to the acre, the average 28 stones; the Belgium-France-Holland region averaged 32—35 stones, with all others, including Scandinavia, Russia and Italy, getting only 18—22 stones to the acre.

At this stage the flax fibre is only comparable to a fleece straight off the sheep — by no means ready for spinning. Much of the fibre is still largely in wads and needs splitting down; some will need untangling and straightening. This specialist task, intermediate between those of the grower—retter and of the spinner, is done by the 'heckler', comparable to the wool-comber. He begins on the 'ruffler' heckle, the coarsest: a fixed board plated with tin and bearing 7 in steel teeth which taper to a fine point. The heckler, taking a strick of rough fibre by the head-ends, spreads out the root-end and, lashing the tips on the heckle, pulls the fibres through the teeth. This action is repeated, working gradually nearer the craftsman's hand, until the fibre is judged acceptable. The strick is reversed and the head-end similarly treated. The worker then moves on to a heckle with 5 in, more closely set teeth, and so on, perhaps using as many as four heckles. Cartwright's 1789 wool-combing machine led to the mechanisation of flax-heckling.

For the finest spinning, the strick will be 'cut' in three, the centre being that used; the two ends are uneven in strength and length, that at the root harsh and woody. The fibres might also be cut just in two parts. The opposite to cut flax is 'long line', the fibre being left complete.

Pliny described how the ancient Egyptians combed out their flax with iron hooks, adding that 'men were not ashamed to prepare it'. Fig.22b, left end, is thought to show flax combing, by Egyptian women. These people distinguished — as is done now — between the fine white inner fibres and the layer outside them, used only for lamp-wicks.

These poorer fibres together with all the inner fibres which are broken in the heckling are now sold in Britain as 'tow'. A lower grade still, including fibre collected up after the scutching stage, goes on sale as *codilla,* apparently from the Latin for the 'tail'.

The smooth, glossy, dressed 'line' is now ready for hand-spinning. But again, if machines are to be used, the flax has to be drawn out into slivers, these combined, re-drawn and so on, innumerable times, until regularised, then finally drawn out and slightly twisted into the roving, ready for mechanical spinning. An average machine count is 150 skeins, of 300 yards each, to a pound, reaching up to twice as fine (chapter 9).

Jute preparation in India

Jute plants are leafy annual shrubs growing to 5—10 ft in height. Long cultivated for home use in the hot moist climate of India, they are raised much as a European flax crop. Cut — not pulled — and then retted, their spectacular scutching contrasts with the sober routine of north-west European commercial agriculture. Having first roughly stripped off most of the unwanted bark, 'the native operator, standing up to his middle in water', in the words of a Victorian spectator, 'next proceeds to wash off: this is done by taking a large handful, swinging it round his head he dashes it repeatedly against the surface of the water . . . then with a dextrous throw he fans it out on the surface . . . and carefully picks off all remaining black spots'. Yield of fibre in this state varied from 5—30 cwt the acre, averaging 13 cwt. The Victorian account noted its cheapness with satisfaction: from 3d to 4/— an *acre* to cultivate, at a time when it reached England at 15/— a *cwt*. Many British merchants were not merely importers but had soon installed factories in Bengal, since industry was able to pay still lower wages there than in Dundee.

Before spinning, jute has always been treated with both oil and water, followed by 14—48 hours fermentation. Early mechanisation used a softening machine, with 12—18 pairs of rollers; it stood in a trough holding a mixture of 1—2 pints oil and 10—15 pints of water to 100 lb of jute.

Phormium, the Maoris' fibre plant

Phormium had long been used in New Zealand when the British arrived in the islands. The individual craftsmanship put unstintedly into the work was producing a yarn recognised at once by the colonists as second only to the abaca of the Philippines. They thus found it profitable to stimulate production of the fibre and export it to Britain. However, when in 1863—4 a particularly severe conflict with the Maoris disrupted supplies, the settlers tried to plant and process the fibre themselves. Chemical retting systems were worked out, machines for stripping the leaves were designed. At length the enterprise was declared a failure, the reason being that the Maoris, by 'wastefully' using only the best fibres — which the machines could not distinguish from the rest — had more or less misled the exporters into believing phormium could be a commercial proposition. The Maoris, needing the yarn only for their own capes and cords and not as a cash crop, had certainly used only the best fibres — but their craftsmanship had also had an important role in getting the most out of the fibres.

Phormium, both wild and planted, grows fronds from ground level for three years, then sends up a 15 ft seed-stalk and dies. The fronds, 3–9 ft long and 2–3 in wide, grow to maturity in six months, so that two crops were cut each year; the central core of immature leaves was left whilst the very outer leaves were discarded as holding poor-quality fibre. A stripping process was used to get at the raw material in the leaves. Only the fibre from the undersides was used by the Maoris. It was cleaned by being drawn over the edge of a shell and then washed in a stream. The resulting silky cream-coloured fibre could then be used like a heavy flax. The closely similar processes used on the other circum-pacific fibre plants — abaca, yucca and agave — may result from human migrations in the prehistoric period.

Cotton in India

'The people, though remarkable for their intelligence at a time when Europe was in a state of barbarism, made no approximation to the mechanical operations of modern times', wrote a cotton expert, a contemporary of William Morris. Until recently, he went on reprovingly, they had done 'but little towards supplying the manufacturers of other countries with the raw material they required'.

The seeds of the many species of cotton plants give fibre, oil, cattle-cake, soap; the stalks, used as thatch, also give a fibre, coarse and spun like jute, or made into paper. The Indians' basic tools, probably used since the settlement at Mohenjo-Daro, have been the separator and the cleaner. The most primitive way of getting the down off the seeds was to put these on a large dished stone and roll an iron bar to and fro over them with the feet; the west rarely uses its feet now as direct tools.

A more advanced method employed the *churka,* a hand-turned mangle which let through the cotton but not the seeds; it is common throughout south-east Asia. Its presence in Italy, as the *manganello,* further supports the idea of the Asiatic hand-wheel entering Europe from the Eastern Mediterranean.

Humboldt, reaching the Upper Orinoco in 1800, found the local people had a still more advanced cotton-separator: 'Wooden cylinders of extremely small diameter through which the cotton passes, and which are made to turn by a treadle'. This doubtless came from the Catholic missionaries, probably Iberian, possibly Italian.

The Asian Indians used the bow (fig.18cd) to clean the cotton. A heap of fibre was spread out and this tool, its string set vibrating by a blow of a mallet, was passed across its surface: the vibrations caused the fibres to start upwards, permanently fluffing themselves and letting go their impurities. Probably hunting bows were first used. For fibre preparation they were employed in prehistoric Asia, Europe and South America; medieval and later Europe used bows for cleaning wool, particularly in the delicate craft of beaver-hat making, and also, as an alternative to the teazle, for raising the nap on finished cloth. The bow is still used by simple craftsmen: the Nigerian tool is only a third as long as that of the hat-trade's 7 ft implement. The cotton, once cleaned, is ready for the hand-spinner.

The pre-mechanisation century of cotton-importing and manufacturing in north-west Europe did not see the development of a specialist craft: the new fibre was processed with the lighter wool and flax tools and incorporated into the domestic and early factory systems. Then came the carding, drawing and spinning machines, designed primarily around the peculiarities of cotton, easy to mechanise. This led in 1792 to Whitney's invention of a saw-based separating engine, or 'gin', this preparing the fibre at a pace commensurate with that of the other machines. Cotton now grows right across the world and is the most commonly spun fibre.

CHAPTER 8

EVOLUTION AND USE OF SPINDLES AND
HAND—TURNED WHEELS

The historical roles of the different techniques were described in the second and third chapters. The techniques themselves will now be explained, at the same time showing their evolution one from the other.

Spinning without a spindle

Fibres have been spun by being rolled between the hands or, as is done with grasses by the Australian aborigenes, upon the upper leg; this second technique was current in Northern Europe up to the second world war. In classical times, thigh-rolling was used to prepare a roving (probably depicted in fig.22b, centre, Egypt). It was most developed in Greece of 600—400 BC, the spinner using a foot-rest and, to protect the leg, a pottery *epinetron* or *onos* (fig.21f, Carpathos); this ornate guard had an imbricated surface, like that of a wool fibre, to stop the greasy wool from slipping as it was rolled.

Spindle techniques

A range of spindles is shown in fig.20; that also in fig.3,

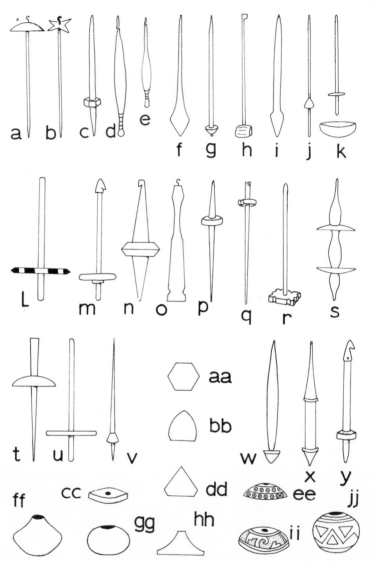

20. *Spindles: Jerusalem, thigh-rolling (ab), Morocco (c), Balearic Islands, single and two-ply (de), Madeira (f), Egypt (g), W Africa, cassava-root whorl (h), Germany (i), Peru (j), India, with coconut shell (k), Australia (l), Denmark, ancient (m), Scottish Highlands (n), Hebrides, author's Jura workshop (o), Roman, London (p), Egypt, c1370 BC (q) Jerusalem (r), France, 1750 (s), Navajo (t), England, modern (u), W Africa (v), Russia (w), France, 1750 (x), S Italy (y). Whorls: Egypt, ancient (aa, bb, dd), Jerusalem (cc), Roman (ee), Britain, Neolithic (ff), Britain, Saxon (gg), Greek, ancient (hh), Aztec (ii), Peru (jj)*

dated to about 1370 BC, is from Akhetakn in Egypt. The stem has usually been of wood, sometimes of bone; the fibres may be attached to the upper end by a slip knot or, better, run through a spiral groove or, best of all, a hook. The whorl can be of wood, stone, a rounded potsherd fragment, clay, metals, a slice of a vegetable, animal and human femur heads, two crossed sticks; it may be enormous, with commensurate stem, like those used by the Salish Indians of Canada for very thick work (fig.22c), or minute, as in silk and muslin spinning in Asia and for cotton in Peru (fig.21h); as can be seen, the whorl may be positioned at any point up the stem, with thigh-spinners, for example, placing it at the top (fig. 20ab); occasionally there are two or even three whorls (fig. 21a). The broader the whorl, compared to the stem, the more the momentum.

At first the fibre was probably just attached to the end of a stick and this rolled on the knee or thigh, easier than rolling the wool itself. The Egyptian women turned back their skirts to expose a hairless surface (fig.22b, right end) — hence probably the Mosaic prohibition on spinning outdoors, especially by moonlight. In Norfolk the leg part of the method was still in use about 1820 AD, though less appealingly: 'the slender spindle receives a whirling motion by being quickly rolled upon a piece of smooth leather, called the trip-skin, fastened upon the thigh of the spinner.' Probably the leather had become smooth by use rather than by design.

The spindle used with the distaff was the most common technique. The fibres might be in the raw state, just a piece of fleece, for example, or could be carded or combed. As has been said, fibres ready for spinning were called *diesse* in Low German — connected with the 'diz' disc — and the stick from which they were dispensed was called in Anglo-Saxon the dis-staff.

The wide range of fixed distaffs (fig.21a-e) divide into the short ones, say a foot long, usually held in the left hand, and those, 3—4ft long, fixed to the waist and supported in the crook of the left arm. The upper end of the evolved distaff had a gripping device such as a cage (c), otherwise flax at least had to be tied round with a string (figs.8,10); the Scandinavian flax distaff used a heckle design to hold and keep separate the fibres (b); a forked stick was usually a guide for rovings (fig.22a, evolved to fig.21e). From the Middle Ages many distaffs were fixed to benches. Those used with wheels were often mounted on these (figs.8,25c), though by no means always (fig.26). By Victorian times many distaffs were free-standing; those for flax had a water-cup halfway up, to avoid the vulgar use of saliva to wet the fingers. The distaff was also known as a 'rock', a word limited in some places to the free-standing type. The re-volving distaff was in use at the end of the Middle Ages for dispensing rovings (fig.21g, Rouen, 1520) but has since been turned into a skein-unwinder (figs. 7, 26).

The technique of spindle-spinning begins with the tieing of a piece of string or spun wool to say the middle of the spindle. Its end spirals upwards round the stem and through the hook, to be knotted — by the beginner at least — to the end of a length of fibre pulled out from the bunch on the distaff. The length may need shaping or teasing a little, according to its state. The spinner, gripping the top of the spindle in the right hand (figs. 10, 26), gives it a strong twist, usually clockwise as seen from above, immediately releasing it so that it hangs on the length of fibre, this still attached to the distaff. Then, for so long as it goes on spinning clockwise on its own, the spinner is free to extend and tease the length of fibre at its upper end, pulling it out from the bundle. The twist will be seen to run up the length as fast as this is pulled free.

A more continuous technique, as in Norfolk, is to roll the spindle on the thigh with the right hand whilst pulling out more fibre with the left. A further refinement: the Tibetans sit on balconies to get longer lengths of yarn before the hanging spindle touches the ground.

Once both adequately spun and uncontrollably long, the length of spun fibre is disengaged from the upper end of the spindle and wound around its body, the position varying with that of the whorl (figs. 3, 10, 22ab). The upper end of the spun fibre is now passed through the hook and the whole process begins again. Breakages are made good by mingling

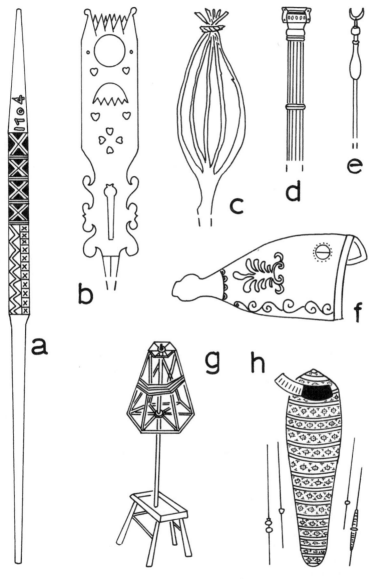

21. *Spinners' aids. Distaffs: Scottish Highlands, 1704 (a), Sweden, flax (b),*
S Italy, tree branch (c), Roman Britain, jet (d), France, 1750 (e),
Pottery knee-guard, Carpathos, 400 BC (f), Revolving distaff and skein
unwinder, Rouen 1525 (g), Pottery case for fine spindles, Peru,
1000 AD (h).

97

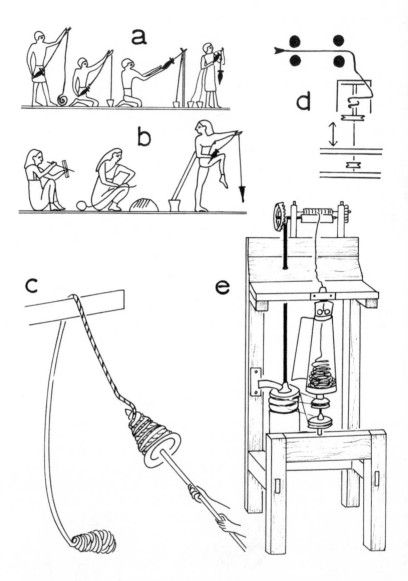

22. Preparation and spinning of rovings. Egypt, 1900 BC (l. to r.): hand
suspension, thigh rolling, forked distaff, two rovings over shoulder (a).
Ancient Egypt (l. to r.): combing flax, thigh rolling a roving (?),
spinning two rovings, over shoulder, on thigh rolled spindles (b).
Salish Indian spinning thick roving over a beam (c). Paul's 1738
design for a four-roller spinning machine with a travelling bobbin (d).
Arkwright's 1775 drawing frame (e).

the fibres of each end and then, holding the mixture firmly between the thumb and forefinger of the left hand, giving the dangling spindle a good twist with the right — then letting the twist *gradually* run up the join by cautiously sliding the fingers upwards. With practice, spindle-spinning soon becomes second nature, as it was to the Paeonian woman in Herodotus' story about King Darius: 'the pitcher of water on her head . . . the horse dragging on her arm . . . she still kept twirling her spindle'.

Although prepared rovings are only essential to machine spinning, some simple spindle-spinners, such as the Egyptians and the Navajos, have rolled rovings, as described in the opening section. Then, to spin this roving, the ball was laid on the ground and drawn by the spinner either through the left hand or over the left shoulder or through the forked distaff, all illustrated by the ancient Egyptians (fig.22ab). If both hands were needed, for heavy work, then an anchored ring was used as a guide, as by the Welsh in the nineteenth century, or perhaps a beam, as by the Salish (fig.22c). Working from rovings made the multiple-spindle technique feasible (fig.22ab) since there was much less to do on each one. European peasants have been recorded using a spindle in each hand, perhaps with rovings.

All the fibres discussed in Chapter 4 have been spun on the spindle, from the nettles of north-west Siberia, recently made into yarn by the Ob-Ougrians — though as the maps show (figs.4, 5), there is little other information on the state of hand-spinning in the USSR — to the pinna of the Mediterranean. Spindle-spinning produces a warp of maximum quality, since the twist can be applied again and again, if needs be, until the fibres are strongly spun. The hand-wheel, as will be seen, gave only a comparatively-loose weak yarn. The spindle thus continued in use for warp in the industrialising countries until the appearance of the treadle-flyer wheel; in remotest Europe it lasted into the nineteen thirties and is still current for both warp and weft in the last non-industrialised parts of the world. However, these are steadily going one by one direct from their own spindle-spinning to the use of machined yarns.

The first step towards the hand-turned wheel can be seen in a single advance made over the distaff method but still within the spindle technique: the use of the bearing. This could have originated by resting a big spindle on the ground, as the Navajos do, and finding it was most easily controlled by continuing to use it in the hole it dug for itself. Or from the need to rest the spindle tip in a smooth shell or bowl because the yarn was so fine that it could not bear the weight of even the lightest of spindles, as in India and Peru (fig.20k). Anyway, eventually the bearing principle was applied to the spindle — to free the hands, it was made to stand in a piece of wood or, as by the Bolivians and Palestinians, to spin between the big and second toes, readily available.

Hand-turned and treadle wheels in Asia

Invented in South-east Asia, the prehistoric age of the hand-wheel hides its evolution. It developed from the spindle, still in use alongside it today. The origin of the hand-wheel was perhaps connected with the similar tool long used for silk-reeling. It seems that all the Asian wheels now known to Europe are of modern construction (figs. 6, 23a).

In the rarely-discussed Indonesian wheel, the spindle is mounted horizontally between a vertical, perforated peg, fixed to the base-board, and the same pair of toes as are used by the Palestinians, for example, as a bearing for the 'foot spindle', though at right angles, of course; otherwise the wheel is similar to the well-known Indian wheels (fig.23a). Possibly, then, the Indonesian represents a transitional stage between spindle and wheel.

A single string passes round both the spindle and the driving wheel, the two mounted on a single board. The Indonesian sits on the ground beside the wheel, the nearest hand able to turn this by a peg fixed to a spoke or by a crank fixed to the axle; the legs are stretched out so that the toes of one foot can support the spindle. The fibres, probably well prepared, run from the tip of the spindle (as

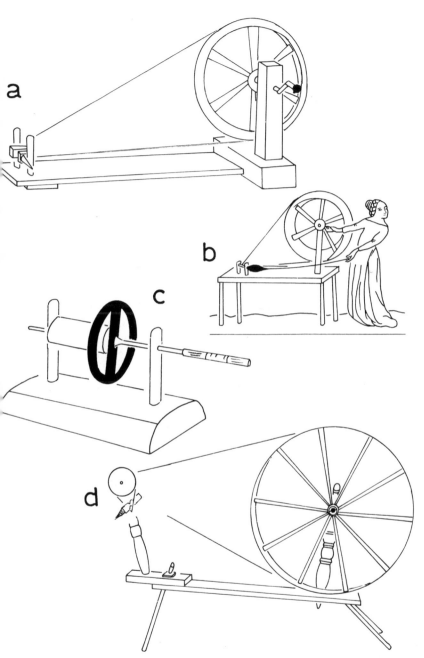

23. Hand-wheels: Indian (a), European, fourteenth century, raised (b),
Tenerife (c), Canadian, with intermediate cog (d).

in fig.23b), this protruding through the two toes, to the other hand. To spin, the wheel is made to turn whilst the length of fibre is held out sideways so that it comes as near as possible to continuing the long axis of the spindle. The flexibility of the toe-mount allows the spindle-tip to be pulled a little towards the spinner, since the arm is otherwise not long enough to spin a good length at the necessary angle without strain to the back. So far there is little or no advance over the results from the unmounted, distaff-hanging spindle. But now, to wind on, the Indonesian spinner has only to bring the yarn round to a right angle to the spindle's long axis — back towards the body, that is — for a further turning action to reel it on the spindle.

Most eastern wheels had *each* end of the spindle mounted on a post (fig.23a), losing the flexibility of the toe-bearing. However, the toes have been used with this wheel too, in a different way: the spinner still sitting, the fibres themselves now ran from the hand to the spindle between the two largest toes, so that the angle-change needed to wind on the yarn could be achieved by a movement of the guide-foot. This can be considered the first move towards the invention of the flyer, though the Asians only went one small stage beyond this.

A minor aspect — often misrepresented in descriptions of the use of hand-wheels — is that, before winding on, a few turns are needed in the opposite direction in order to take off the already-spun yarn spiralling around the outer end of the spindle. The yarn is to be wound around the inner half of the protruding part of the spindle and these outer few inches, unless taken off and replaced at the inner end, would otherwise simply loosen, bunch up and spoil the shape and firmness of the oval of spun fibre (fig.23b). The actual winding-on is most easily done in the same direction as for the 'backing-off' just described, by keeping the wheel going, but it could be done in the same direction as for spinning.

The standard modern Indian wheel (fig.23a) is about a foot across. The Chinese wheel, like the Japanese — this possibly now decreasingly used in this highly industrialised state — is larger, over 2ft in diameter. The Chinese wheel may have two spindles, these mounted overhead, and is often made from two parallel sets of spokes cross-joined by cords, with a woven driving-belt (fig.6). This Chinese rim was apparently in use in eighteenth-century Sweden.

About 1640 AD the Chinese independently invented the treadle (fig.25d); it is distinct from the European version, in use for a century by then. Both the spinner's feet rest on this treadle, one on each side of its supporting fulcrum. There are three spindles, sometimes very long. In this case, the spinner sits in line with the long axis of the spindles, so that the spinning action is without strain. The winding-on is now achieved by altering the angle of the yarn's approach to the spindle with a hand-held stick — the second stage in the invention of the flyer, the first being the toe-guide. It can be noted that the wheel-spindles arrangement of this model is remarkably similar to that of the twisting wheels once used in European rope-walks.

Another recent Asian model mounts the three spindles at the side of the wheel, at the height of the axle; each spindle has its own driving band; presumably it is treadle-powered and used with a stick-guide. These two models represent the maximum Asian technology in hand-spinning. As will be seen, they fall short of the European Saxony wheel by the absence of the mounted, horse-shoe flyer, since the guide-stick does not allow continuous spinning; on the other hand, the Saxony wheel never used more than two spindles.

The hand-turned wheel in Europe

The advent of the hand-wheel in medieval Europe has been discussed in Chapter Two. The spinner stands 'or, rather, runs backwards and forwards', wrote *The Book of English Trades* in 1824. In spite of Velasquez's painting of 1658 (fig. 7), many European wheel-spinners were standing at the beginning: fig. 23b shows a fourteenth-century scene. In the name of production, the working spinner covered about 20 miles a day during the eighteenth century.

Small wheels seem to have been rare in Europe; they

were revived for table spinning in the eighteenth century (fig. 25a). Most early European models had medium-sized wheels; raised on legs, this ruled out the eastern foot-techniques, if these were in fact ever known in the west. Then, after a few centuries, industrialisation expanded the wheel to gigantic size (fig. 1, background); the diameter reached 5 ft, the rim 6 inches wide and one-eighth of an inch thick. The length of the mounting board was increased, with the spindle-end legs removed in some wheels, to give the maximum working distance between spinner and spindle. The great momentum allowed the spinner to leave the wheel and run out sideways, each time producing as much as 6 ft of yarn. A typical European factory had a row of bench-stock cardmen supplying prepared wool to a row of darting and bobbing hand-spinners.

Although the treadle-flyer or Saxony wheel had been invented by 1530, it was the hand-turned wheel, with nothing to recommend it except its cheaper cost, which was installed by the early manufacturers. Since they could only spin loosely, they were put to make woollen weft, using short-fibred wool, and cotton yarns. Woollen warp, long-fibred, together with flax and hemp, were all spun under contract by outside spinners in the last phase of the domestic system — thus overlapping with the early factory phase — on spindles or on Saxony wheels. In Scandinavia, a smaller hand-wheel was used for cotton than for wool. Both medium and large hand-wheels are said to continue in use in Ireland. A recent Canary Island wheel (fig.23c) used a direct drive to the spindle and a wooden cylinder for momentum; either a guide-stick or two operators appear needed for effective spinning.

Within the class of hand-turned wheels there is one interesting innovation. The Canadian model used by the early settlers (fig.23d) had an intermediate cog between the driving wheel and the spindle, increasing the spinning speed. This would have allowed the hired spinner to run even faster.

The hand-wheels had a wide variety of names in Europe. In Britain alone they were called 'great', 'muckle' and 'long', 'one-thread', 'Jersey', 'farm', 'wool', 'walking' and 'bobbing'. Many, replaced by the Saxony model, went on to the role of bobbin-winders for weaving, recalling their likely original connection with silk-reeling. The essence of the hand-wheel technique can be experienced by wedging a 6 in wooden peg in the intake hole of a treadle-flyer wheel, then using it as a hand-wheel.

CHAPTER 9

EVOLUTION AND USE OF THE FLYER—
TREADLE WHEEL

The inventions of flyer and treadle, now almost 500 years old, brought the spinning wheel virtually to its present form (fig.25bc). Diderot's 1750 *Encyclopédie* illustrates the parts, using a French wheel which could also be turned by hand (fig.24); the spoke stumps were presumably to increase momentum. This model has some resemblance to the contemporary English table-wheel, with flyer (fig.25a).

The spinner should experiment to find the most comfortable working position. One posture is to put the left foot on the treadle (op) and left side towards the spindle assembly (mounted between s and t). The beginner, who should already have learnt to spin on a spindle, should now practice continuous treadling of the wheel, without trying to spin. The hand gives the wheel a turn and the foot then takes up the action. The aim should be to achieve a steady rhythm. Since the treadling speed governs the rate at which the raw fibres must be fed to the spindle, the slowest pace at which the wheel can be kept turning should be practised.

Once the treadling has become more or less unconscious, the hand actions can be learned. Assuming the left side forward, then the left hand will pull the fibres from the right, the raw material lying behind this, around the spinner's right hip. The alternative use of the distaff is much as in spindle-spinning (figs.25c, 26, wheels used with distaffs). A piece of string or other yarn is tied firmly round the

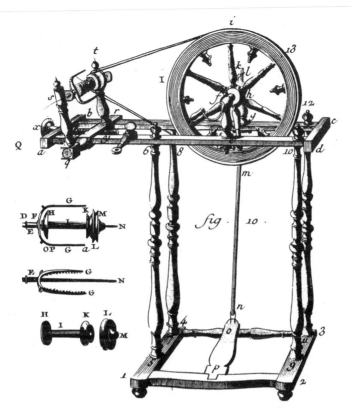

24. The parts of a spinning wheel (French, framed, 1750)

middle of the bobbin (HK), then run around the nearest hook on either flyer arm (G) and brought out through the intake hole (D) — this starting yarn thus follows the course of the already-spun yarn in the diagram (Q). The end of the unspun fibre is knotted to the starting yarn; the fibres may be raw, carded or combed or in a roving.

The spinner treadles *slowly,* turning the big wheel. This, by means of a string, doubled and thus inevitably crossed, turns two cogs in the spindle assembly. The smaller cog (K) is part of the bobbin; the latter revolves freely on the spindle (DN). The larger cog (LM) is fixed to the spindle and, since the flyer (GG) is fixed to this too, this larger cog drives the flyer. Because it has the smaller driving cog, the bobbin moves faster than the flyer: the starting yarn, running between the two, is thus drawn towards and wound round the bobbin. The unspun fibres follow it, going from the spinner's hands towards the intake hole (D) and eventually out along the flyer arm and onto the bobbin. The twist is imparted to the fibres between the moment they leave the spinner's grip and the moment at which they start along the flyer arm.

The spinner has to prepare the fibres simultaneously — according to the thickness and regularity required — and at the speed demanded by the bobbin, this in turn governed, subject to a minimum, by the treadling rate. Once a continuous flow can be produced, the spinner can work on until the bobbin is full, only stopping occasionally to change to a new hook on the flyer arm, to fill the bobbin evenly.

Leonardo's travelling flyer, designed around 1490, about a decade after the first flyer appeared, aimed to spread the yarn along the bobbin automatically, thus allowing fully-continuous spinning (fig.9). In this case the bobbin was driven by the large cog, in the centre, and the flyer by the smaller cog to the immediate left of the large one; the left-end cog was also linked to the flyer by being fixed to the spindle and, since it revolved in a reciprocating fork — shown in the upper drawing and in the complete machine, in the centre — the flyer moved along the bobbin, at an appropriate speed. However, it is not clear how the flyer's driving cog was to remain aligned with its big wheel. Leonardo's design used two driving wheels, apparently made of solid discs of wood linked by wooden pegs, a little like the Chinese wheels. His comparatively-complex design was as near to a machine as to a hand-craft tool — and the travelling flyer was not actually built until the textile trade became mechanised three centuries later. In 1976 a model based on fig.9 has been built by a cabinet-maker for the Helmshore Local History Society (Lancashire).

A small problem with the flyer wheel is that, as the bobbin fills, so each of its turns winds on a greater circumference of yarn — but, the spindle's turning speed staying the same, the yarn becomes progressively less spun. This can be compensated by withholding the fibres a little, the driving band being loosened so that the bobbin cog can slip below it in response to the resistance from the spinner's hands. A peg (fig.24x) adjusts the tension of the band.

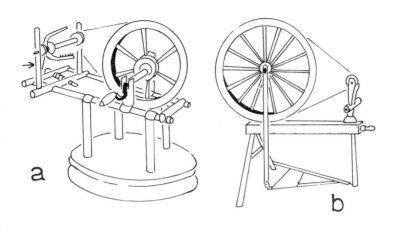

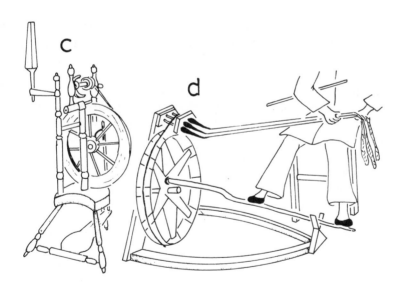

25. *Advanced wheels: English table, with flyer, 1750 (a), Swedish, plain (b), Icelandic, ornate (c), Chinese, fulcrum treadle, three spindles, guide-stick, cotton (d).*

Alternatively, if the bobbin is not winding on adequately, it *may* be that the bands need tightening.

The beginner will usually find the fibres becoming over-tight, kinked and not passing smoothly on to the bobbin. This over-spinning problem is normally caused by the over-fast treadling coupled with a too-slow release by the hands of the prepared fibres; the kinked yarn will, in turn, be fouling the intake hole and the hooks, thus aggravating the situation. The vicious circle is best ended by simply un-tangling everything and starting again.

Europe's treadle-flyer wheels all work in much the same way. The oldest in existence, dating from about 1600, is in Belfast Museum. It is the compact 'vertical' type, in which the spindle assembly is mounted above the wheel (fig.25c). The 'horizontal' alternative, rather more common, has the wheel to the right of the spinner (figs. 24, 25b, 26). Both types have been called 'Saxony' wheels, since they were designed or at least developed there. As they spread, each region gave them a new name, usually that of the immediate-source area. The vertical Irish 'castle' type, distinctive, mounts the spindle assembly below the wheel. There has been wide variation in the angle of the base or 'table' of the horizontal wheels. Framed wheels were common in France, Germany and Italy (figs. 24, 26). A minute portable wheel, for use strapped to the wrist, was made in 1768. The Scandinavians in particular have favoured a large wheel, for its greater momentum and thus greater control in treadling (fig. 25b).

Wheels with two spindle assemblies, requiring great dexterity, were in use into the last century in many parts of Europe. An Austrian model, mounting the spindles above, in the style of the Chinese treadle wheel (fig. 25d), had four grooves in the rim of the wheel to take the four driving bands. These wheels were probably only used for prepared flax, like the triple spindles of the ancient Egyptian virtuosi.

A variation which has recently been revived is the friction bobbin, used by the current Ashford wheel, this made in New Zealand. The most common Saxony wheel had the bobbin driven forwards by its own cog, as described.

However, on many only the spindle-flyer linkage was positively turned by a band — in this case a single string — and the bobbin was simply dragged round by the flyer, to which it was joined by the yarn. To ensure the bobbin kept a slower pace, friction was used: a loop of string went around the bobbin's cog — otherwise used to drive it — and to a simple tensioning peg. Effectively, the flyer wound the yarn round the bobbin. Old wheels of this type have often lost the peg and string, but the peg-hole in the table remains; the distaff's mounting hole, also usually empty, was larger. These bobbins can equally well be driven by the big wheel — provided their cog is aligned with this, not the case with the Ashford, for example.

There are two more possibilities. Wheels have been made with friction flyers (fig. 25a, the friction string indicated), these revolving more slowly than the bobbins. Finally, wheels were tried with driven flyers turning faster than driven bobbins (see also figs. 9, 22d).

For those building wheels, the friction band has two advantages. On the bobbin it can be used to compensate for the accelerating winding-on speed by being gradually tightened and thus slowing it down — the normal tensioning device affects both bobbin and flyer. Flexibility is the other advantage: only one cog needs to be aligned with the big wheel. Thus, the flyer cog can be attached directly to the back of the flyer (perhaps done on model in fig. 25a), rather than to the spindle, a harder task. Additionally, an ancient, warped wheel is most easily aligned to a single cog.

The Saxony wheel, then, gradually replaced the hand-turned wheel throughout Europe and its colonies (fig. 4), lasting into this century in the remote settlements; the horizontal type is said to be still in use, for flax, in Donegal. The Saxony has been used for warp and weft spinning from a wide range of fibres. The 'Jura' wheel described in the next chapter adapts the Saxony design, specifically the Irish castle variant, to the still wider needs of the modern hand-spinner.

Spinning direction

If the wheel — or spindle — is turned in a clockwise direction, then the twist on a length of yarn, removed from the bobbin and held vertically, will be found to run from the right down to the left, like the centre bar of the letter Z; an anti-clockwise motion produces the opposite, like the centre stroke on an S. The spinner cannot change direction within a bobbinful. Flax rotates anti-clockwise when wetted and the early Egyptians did S-spin. Cotton can rotate in either direction but if Z-spun washes well and if S-spun tends to come apart.

Animal fibres do not rotate when wet. Felting properties are highest when warp and weft are each spun in different directions.

The wide variation in practice suggests that, beyond the fundamentals just covered, the direction is unimportant. The Scandinavian Bronze Age seemingly preferred S-warps and Z-wefts. The Romans spun almost entirely Z-twist yarns in their northern provinces but almost all S-twist in the eastern territories. Analysis of late-Medieval Danzig cloth gave, warp first (by century): 70% Z–Z and 30% Z–S (tenth), almost 100% Z–S and some S–S (eleventh), 35% Z–Z, almost 65% Z–S and a little S–S (twelfth) and almost 100% Z–S (thirteenth).

‘ Plying the spun fibres

Plying, comparatively monotonous work, is only necessary if the single yarn is considered to be too uneven or too weak, likely in the case of warp spinning. A two-ply is made by taking the ends of two batches of spun yarn and putting them through the spinning process together. However, the direction of the twist should now be the reverse of that used for the original spinning. If in skeins, then the yarns are best plyed from two revolving distaffs (fig.21g); if in balls, then each is best in a separate container, on the floor, such as the Highlanders' *mudag.*

Spindle plying is preferably done on a heavier model than for the spinning, as in the Balearics (fig.20de). Various countries have brought the two yarns over a beam and turned the spindle with both hands, as the Salish did for heavy spinning (fig.22c). As an example, the Navajos made four-ply for their blankets. Up to 72-ply yarn has been spun on the spindle.

In India three long spindles were used, their upper ends with tapering cage-like enlargements. The worker stuck two, their cages each wound round with single yarn, in the ground, near-vertically. Taking the yarn end from each, he tied these to the cage of the third, stuck in his belt. Guiding the yarns with his left hand, he turned the belt spindle with his right. The purpose of the cage, used only in this way in India, was to obtain a fast winding rate by increasing the circumference of the spindles; solid spindles of that size would have been very heavy. The two ground-embedded spindles are simply slender versions of the revolving distaff, in use for dispensing rovings and for plying in Europe of the Middle Ages (fig.21g).

The hand-turned wheels, unable to spin 'hard' yarns, were not good at plying either. Diderot illustrated a hand-turned factory device which took the loosely plied yarn from the spinners and, a dozen bobbins at a time, tightened the twist; this was combined with the first stage in preparing the yarn for warping on the loom. Possibly the Norfolk spindle-spun yarn of the next century was plied in the same way, since the men who did it were called 'winders'. The Saxony wheel plied all the yarns of the past satisfactorily.

The reel

The woollen chains which linked the industry-feeding spinner to her wheel also shackled her to the counting reel. As a device for controlling the output of piece-workers it was far ahead of its time: the spinner was paid by the hank spun, the weaver by the hank woven. The reel did however have a technical function in the gauging and ordering of

26. *Spinning in a French* salon, *1750 (l. to r.): spindle and distaff, skein unwinder and winder, framed Saxony wheel and distaff*

yarns and cloths.

There have always been skeiners, of course — the fore-arm or, for the Navajos, the leg below the bent knee. Or a stick with two cross-bars at right-angles to each other (fig. 7, under the wheel). The simplest revolving skeiner, perhaps dating from the seventeenth century, was like a broadened Chinese hand-wheel. It can be seen in Diderot's engraving of 1750 (fig.26): the woman second from the right is skeining up a bobbin spun by the woman on the extreme right. Since they are obviously spinning for pleasure, in their drawing room, the reel has no counting device; their status is indicated by the maid, extreme left, who spins flax, standing, on the humble spindle. The remaining woman is making a ball out of a skein, on the tool evolved from the revolving distaff.

The statutory British yarn-counters of the eighteenth century were of two sizes, measured around the circumference of the arms: 2½ yards for flax, but 1½ yards and then, by the end of the century, 2 yards for wool. Considering the flax counter (figs.11, 27), in England, each turn was called a 'thread' and 120 turns made a 'lea' or skein of 300 yards or so. The number of skeins weighing a

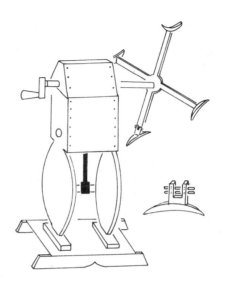

27. Hammer reel, Sweden

pound gave the yarn count. Ten skeins made a 'hank' and twenty hanks a 'bundle'. The woollen skein had to be 256 yards, the worsted skein 560 yards, the latter the basis of the yarn counts given, by breed of sheep, in Chapter 5. With the cotton industry developing, Arkwright made a counter geared to skeins of 840 yards to the pound. The details varied from country to country.

The yarn was wound straight off the spinning-wheel bobbin on to the aligned counter. The gearing below grudgingly recorded the accumulating 'threads'. The completion of a 'skein' was signalled by a variety of devices: by the release of a wooden spring on the Scottish 'click' reel (fig.11), by a hammer blow in Sweden (fig.27), on a dial in Arkwright's model. The skein was removed by relaxing the tension by collapsing an arm (figs.11, 27; in the first, the bulge on the turning arm slides, the arm being hinged underneath). The spinner returned yet again to her wheel.

The technical evolution of the first spinning machines

'As the prepared mass regularly passes through these

rowlers . . . other rowlers . . . moving proportionately faster . . . draw the rope, thread or sliver in any degree of fineness', thus ran Paul's patent of 1738, its principle shown in fig.22d. It is simply a Saxony wheel assembly preceded, for the fibre-thinning hitherto done by the spinner's hands, by two pairs of rollers which, moving at different speeds, stretch out the fibres whilst these are between them. Leonardo had proposed a horizontal travelling flyer — Paul's bobbin was to fill itself evenly by moving up and down due, optimistically, to 'the motion of the frame'. The arrows (fig.22d) indicate the travelling distance. Paul's diagram shows a faster flyer than bobbin, as in Leonardo's machine. In 1758 Paul patented a simpler model: the drawing out of the fibres would be done by the mere demand action of the bobbin, thus replacing the second set of rollers; the bobbin had of course to move faster than the remaining pair of rollers.

Paul's 1738 design was taken over thirty years later by Arkwright for his drawing frame (fig.22e), already described, and spinning machine (fig.12). Arkwright's first spinning engine, 1769, used four pairs of rollers for each roving. These rollers revolved at relative speeds of I: 1.17: 1.33: 6.25, reading from back to front, of course; the upper rollers were leather-covered, the lower were of horizontally-ribbed wood; the four rows of four pairs were pressed together by weights hanging on the ends of the upper-roller spindles. The bobbins were friction-slowed against flyers driven by cogs below; there were originally four flyer-bobbin assemblies (only two remain in fig.12). The 32 rollers and four flyer-cogs were turned — the former through cogs, the latter through a belt — by a large wheel, also missing, mounted horizontally on the tip of the back lower triangle, far left (fig.12). And this large wheel was turned by a horse.

Paul's designs had not materially increased output over that of the spinning wheels — cheap to build and to operate — and in practice his machines' performance was made the worse by their tendency to break the threads. But Arkwright's machines processed the fibres more gradually: he fed in slightly-twisted and thus stronger rovings and, increasing the rollers to four pairs, drew out the fibres more slowly. As explained, his drawing frame was needed to make the rovings; its front rollers turned at 3.4 times that of the back.

About 1775 Arkwright built a more advanced water-powered machine, with eight spindles and efficient travelling bobbins, known as the 'water-frame'. Arkwright, then, took the basic design from Paul, improved on it and made the functioning models that led on to the wide use of the roller-based machine — fundamentally built on the design of the Saxony wheel.

The hand-turned wheel had, in the meantime, been developed into a second line of successful spinning machines. Presumably it was the trade's lack of enthusiasm for Paul's machines that led Hargreaves, in 1767, to imitate the inferior hand-wheel; had Arkwright's machine been known by then, Hargreaves' engine, or 'jenny', might never have been invented. Nevertheless, its peculiar features were to be incorporated into a third and most important line of machines which was to begin in 1772—9.

Hargreaves' first model was said to have been inspired by the sight of a spinning wheel which had fallen on its side but was still turning. His original version had eight near-vertical spindles powered by a hand-wheel at right angles to them; the number of spindles was later increased (fig.14, simplified). The thinning action of the spinner's hands — and of Paul's 'rowlers' — was done by two wooden bars (a) running across the machine. To begin, the prepared fibre slubbings (beneath, b) were passed between the bars and attached to the spindle tips (c), just as in the hand-turned wheels. The two bars were now made to clamp together, gripping the fibre ribbons, and then were moved away from the spindles (reaching the position in fig.14). This drew out the fibres. At the same time the spindles had begun to turn, already giving coherence to the fibres and thus strengthening them against the strain of the retreating 'draw' clamp. This was now at the end of its backwards movement but the spindles continued to spin the fibres. Next — by an action which has to be done with all hand-wheels, from the Indonesian onwards — the spindles were given a few reverse turns, the backing-off to clear their tips of yarn; this was done with a treadle-activated width-running metal rod (d) which was pressed down on the yarn just short of the tips of the near-vertical spindles. Finally, the draw-clamp travelled forwards again to the beginning as, simultaneously, the spindles wound on the spun yarn. The draw clamp now opened and moved *part* of the way back, allowing fresh slubbing lengths to pass through it — then it closed and the whole process began again.

The third line of machines was begun by Crompton's 'mule', hybrid between those of Hargreaves and Arkwright. The rollers and the reciprocating draw-clamp were combined to produce a more efficient machine than either. The jenny, like its ancestor, could only spin soft wefts; the mule was also designed to spin wefts. The water-frame spun hard firm warps. All these machines were basically made for cotton-spinning and then adapted to other fibres.

The spinners and weavers repeatedly broke into the factories and smashed the jennies and the water-frames. However, the 'lawless rabble' was always 'dispersed' and the inventions went on, in the words, including emphasis, of a Victorian writer, to be *'universally* productive of wealth and enjoyment.'

Workshop output

The following hourly production, based on ancient records and modern experiments, is for fine yarns and includes, in the case of hand-spinning, about fifteen minutes spent on the fibres' preparation. The normal range for spindle spinning is 60-120 yards, exceptionally 50% more; the hook spindle has given the best yield. The hand-turned wheel has been recorded as doing 300-400 yards, presumably working at a frenzied pace, since the continuous-output Saxony wheel only averages 350-450 yards — from about 2 oz of wool — or 500 yards with two spindles assemblies. Paul's rollers also produced 500 yards. Change began with the jenny, 2000 yards an hour, powered and controlled by one man.

Domestic system output has been recorded by weight

of wool-pack. The spindle spinners only did a couple of pounds in a 70-hour week. Wheel-spinners in the more advanced zones of the Scottish Highlands were left 3 lb of wool a week each by the merchants. The last Harris tweed spinners reached a pound a day.

About 1800 the Welsh women, carding and spinning coarse yarn on hand-wheels, were said to be dealing with 9 lb of wool a day, the equivalent of three good fleeces from the mountain sheep. The raw wool was worth 9-12d a pound and they were paid 2d a pound for their work; another estimate was that, darting to and fro, they covered a mile a penny.

Fine spinning has always been admired. An Egyptian mummy shroud had 540 linen threads, spindle spun, across an inch of fabric. Roman Britain produced wool yarn 'comparable to the spider's web'. In 1800 a Lincoln woman spun out a pound of wool to 95 miles and, half a century later, an 84-year-old Irish woman drew a pound of flax out to 130 miles. However, also at the Great Exhibition of 1851, there was shown a pound of cambric linen yarn hand-spun to 278 miles. It was said that the Cambrai spinners could only get this out of the flax by working in damp cellars; the yarn was so fine that, in the gloom, they were guided by touch alone. Cambric yarn then sold at up to £240 a pound.

Lastly, an idea of the spinner's place, about 1600, in the sequence of craftsmen involved in the making of a piece of cloth. At the time of the overlap of the guild, domestic and proto-factory systems, there were twenty workers to a loom, in England: three or four spinners and the rest preparers, dyers, carders and combers, the weaver, cloth fullers and shearers and so on. Two centuries later a 240 lb wool-pack gave a week's stocking-making work to 10 combers, 100 spinners and winders, 60 weavers and almost 30 other craftsmen, at least 50 man-hours on each raw pound of wool and, assuming 40% loss in preparation, a good 80 hours on each pound's weight of stockings. The first century of mechanisation reduced by four-fifths the man-hours needed on a piece of cloth.

The work can also be seen in terms of cloth length, as in the following analysis of the production of 30 yards of Harris tweed at a time when the whole process was carried out by a man and his wife in their home. Starting with about 50 lb of raw wool, 60 hours were spent on preparations, 160 hours carding, 240 hours spinning, 60 hours weaving, 20 hours finishing. This gave 30 yards of cloth weighing as many pounds, at 18 hours to the yard.

Considered in terms of the hourly wages of the nineteen seventies, these are expensive stockings and cloth. Modern commercial craftworkers can reduce on the time and energy used by developing and inventing methods and equipment. Home and community clothworkers will additionally save, probably, by not wanting their products to be too 'refined'. The gap is further bridged by the generally greater beauty and longer life of hand-made pure-fibre textiles. For the rest, the potential craftsman — simultaneously on the threshold, perhaps, of alternative society — has the varied opinions of the opening chapter to reassure him.

CHAPTER 10

MAKING A SPINNING WHEEL

A spinner's workshop needs little but light. The writer uses part of a converted stable (fig.35, foreground) for dyeing, spinning and weaving, and also for wood-turning, on a treadle lathe. The following instructions for making the spinner's tools are intended for those with some experience of wood-working — and of improvisation.

Spindles

These have a use as learning aids, since they give beginners practice in teasing out the fibres without the simultaneous task of treadling a wheel. The turned one-piece type is the strongest . . . spindles do sometimes fall to the ground. However, a large whorl, giving a high momentum, is more easily made separately from the stem, to which it then has however to be fitted.

Cards

This description (based on fig.28) of the way cards were made in France about 1750 is only intended as a guide. To begin, a rectangle of well-tanned goat or calf skin was

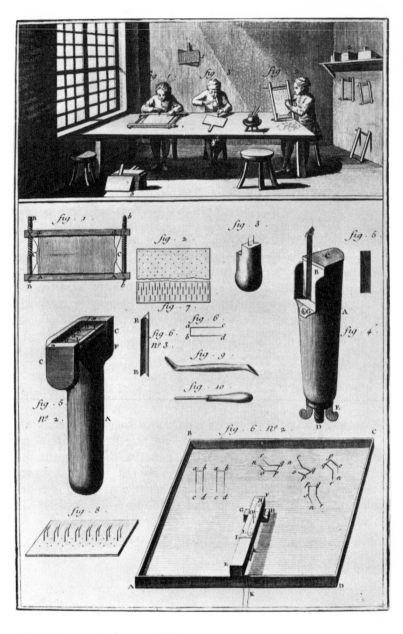

28. Making cards, France, 1750

stretched on a frame called the *panteur* (BBbb); when taut, the skin should be the size of the wooden backing of the intended card. It was held by cords on each short side and by hooks on the long sides. A pumice stone is used to thin and soften the skin, according to the rigidity required of the teeth. Thin places are pasted over with paper or thin skin.

Next the teeth holes are pierced, in a quincunx pattern (upper scene I and lower 2), by a double awl or *fourchette* (lower 3); the tool's notch is to take the index finger. Some used multiple-point implements. The pattern should be marked out in advance. The brass-wire teeth, their thickness, elasticity and so on depending upon their future work, were next cut in a gauge (4). The iron gauge-plate (C) could be adjusted in the vertical through a long screw (D) when the butterfly nut (E) was turned; the flattened bundle of wires, 50-100 tied together, lay in the iron-faced recess (B); the lengths (5) were now cut off with a stroke of a chisel, to an average of 1½ inches.

These brass teeth were next bent in the *doubleur* (5, No.2), its body of wood and upper parts of iron. To achieve the desired shape (6 abcd), the upper end of the bender bears a triangular-section piece of iron, the *goutière* (6, No.3, EE): it is suspended in the *doubleur* so that the gap underneath is the same thickness as the wire. This slot is now filled with cut wires; each sticks out (FDL). These wires are then bent up, over and down until they touch the base at the back — the triangular section of the front gutter means that the teeth's second bend, 45°, springs back to a right angle when released (6abcd).

The staple-shaped *points*, as they were now called, went next to a tray (6, No.2). The essence of the contraption in the middle is the *crocheux*, a metal plate (LM) which had holes the width and depth — in the wood underneath — of the legs of the staples. The staples were then put in one by one and bent to their final shape (nopqr).

Next the staples were passed through the stretched skin (upper scene 2, lower 8) and held temporarily by a layer of glue on the back (7). The teeth were now sharpened with a fine stone, not the obvious point at which to do this. Those now muddled, not surprisingly, were re-aligned with the *fendoir* (9), one end rounded, the other pointed. Any wrong angles were corrected with a handled tube, the *dresseur* (10), pushed over the offending tooth and this then bent; the tube's bore was that of the wire.

Lastly, the skin was nailed to the handled backing, of beech wood (upper scene, foreground heap). It had to be kept tightly stretched and so was presumably nailed to the backing whilst still on the stretcher-frame, then released. The edges were covered with strips of skin, nailed on in turn.

Armed with the ability to make the essential toothed fabric, the spinner can go on more easily to design and build a more advanced hand-carder. Possibilities include the bench-stock, swinging and roller types (Chapter 6).

Building a Jura wheel

Antique wheels are part of the *mystique* of spinning — precisely the part which gives the craft its nostalgic back-to-nature reputation and slows down its re-acceptance both as a purposeful occupation and as part of a rational way of life. Old wheels are also a staple of the antique trade, their price rising steeply as would-be spinners sadly compete for them with wealthy tourists. And, separated from their rose-tinted aura, many are quite ugly; the ornate bulbous turning would not now be generally acceptable on a piece of furniture. Lastly, once bought, the old wheels often work badly and, in any case, their design does not meet all of the needs of the modern spinner.

Nor do any of the modern commercial wheels, since all have the basic design and range of the Saxony wheel. The simplest and cheapest, the Ashford kit, costs about £60 (1978); running smoothly on nylon bearings, it is a friction-bobbin machine built of silver beech. With prices ranging to around £100, there are then many retail models faithfully imitating the ornamentation of the eighteenth and nineteenth century wheels and, sometimes less successfully, the working parts; there have been Saxony copies for sale with bobbin and flyer cogs the same size, so that the yarn could not have been wound on.

It is most satisfying to make one's own wheel. Alternative wheels have of course been designed and built, but, as far as the author knows, the plans have not been made

29. Jura wheel

generally available; in Britain, a member of the Scoraig community, on the West Highland coast, is said to use one of his own construction. The prototype offered here (figs.29-34), designed by the author in 1975, is comparatively quickly and simply built; in particular it replaces the traditional, complex, welded-steel spindle by a tube screwed to a wooden rod. It can be made entirely from re-cycled materials; if the parts have to be bought, then the total cost is at present about £12. The solid design uses more wood than a traditional wheel, especially if this were made without turning; though heavier, it does not take up noticeably more floor space. Its size is partially linked to its capacities but could be reduced, to some extent, at different points; its weight makes it very stable in use. Ideas for improvement are listed below.

From a working point of view, the Jura design has the following advantages:

1) It can spin not only the usual yarn diameters but goes up to ¾ in, perhaps the maximum generally needed at present. This is valuable to the commercial spinner in particular: most raw materials, especially wool, are cheap compared to industrial wages, so that strong, thick hand-made textiles compete better, considering only prices, with the usually-meagre machine products.

2) The wheel has a bobbin capacity of about a pound (fig. 29, one ball), giving a long flow of spinning, even of the thickest yarn.

3) The easy passage of the fibres makes the wheel fast to work and, above all, easy to learn on. This is judged by results at the author's teaching workshop in Edinburgh (Appendix 5).

4) The treadle tends to return to the top of its circuit as it stops, making re-starting a little quicker.

5) The inwards-tapering extension to the flyer cog returns a wandering driving-band to its groove.

6) The two-speed bobbin, reversible, gives a choice of winding-on rates.

The elements of the Jura wheel are given in the following tables, the letters identifying the parts in diagrams 30, 33-4.

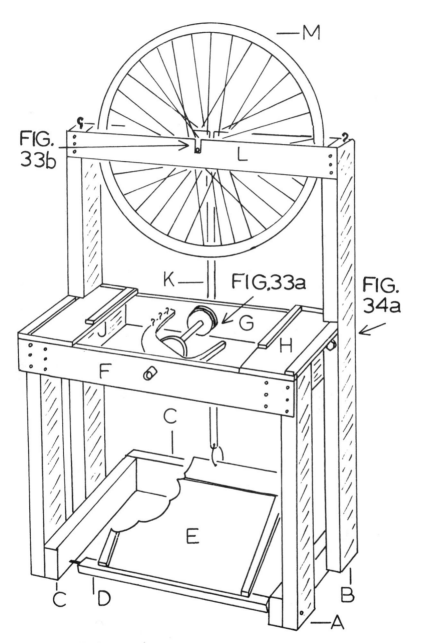

FIG.
33b

FIG.33a

FIG.
34a

30 Jura wheel, diagram

127

	Name & quantity	Description (inches)
A	Front upright (2)	26 x 3¾ x 1⁷/8
B	Back upright (2)	44 x 3¾ x 1⁷/8
C	Base bar (3)	21½ x 3¾ x 1⁷/8
D	Treadle bar (l)	20½ x 1¼ x 1¼. Mounted on steel pins 6″ long and ¼″ diameter (eg headless nails). Push in through holes right through AC
E	Treadle (1)	18 x 18 x ¾ (thickness varies with wood — oak in fig. 29). It is cut away in fig.30 to show back base bar.
F	Front bar (1)	29 x 3¾ x ¾
G	Back bar (1)	29 x 3¾ x ¾
H	Trays (2)	14⁷/8 x 5½ x ½, with strip edging
J	Side bars (2)	14 x 3¾ x 1⁷/8
K	Treadle rod (1)	34 x 1 (eg broomstick) with string
L	Top bars (2)	29 x 2¾ x ½
M	Bicycle wheel	23½ diameter, 1½ rim, 3³/8 hub-to-hub outside width (prefer large, heavy, old-style wheel)
—	Bobbin-flyer assembly	Fig.33a
—	Wheel hub-crank ''	Fig.33b
—	Tensioning device	Fig.34a

Table 5 : Description of frame, Jura wheel

	Name & quantity	Description (inches)
N	Tube (1)	Copper, etc. 4 × ¾ (interior diameter)
O	Collar (1)	Leather, rubber etc. 7/8 (interior diameter)
P	Flyer (1)	2¼ across screws, maximum length 8½, width 7½, thickness 1 (can taper to ½ at tips). Three brass hooks, ½ interior diameter.
Q	Bobbin (1)	7 over-all, shank 5½, cogs ¾ each. Shank diameter 1. Cog outer diameters 3, drive diameters 2¼ , 2½. Leave cog-notches unpolished.
R	Flyer cog (1)	1½ along turning axis, 3 diameter at each end. Drive diameter 2¾ . Leave notch and tapering surface unpolished. Squared extension 2 × 2.
S	Spindle (1)	13 long. Zone 1, circular, ¾ diameter; 2, square-section, 5/8; 3, circular ½ diameter; 4, square-section, 3/8; 5, circular 3/8
T	Treadle return (2)	Strip of strong rubber (eg. car inner-tube)

Table 6 : Bobbin-flyer assembly, Jura wheel

Name & quantity		Description (inches)
U	Hub of bicycle wheel	3 3/8
V	Retainer	Leather, 2¾ x 1½
W	Crank plate	Steel, 3 x 1 x 1/8
X	Crank bolt	Steel, 2 x 5/16. With loose washer and locking nuts (three in fig.33b — the outer one is as much a spacer, as Note 3)
Y	Wheel spindle	5 5/16 x 5/16. With locking nuts (2)

Table 7: Wheel hub-crank assembly, Jura wheel

31 Jura wheel, flyer-bobbin assembly

Construction notes

1) All wood except PQRS can be of soft species, screwed or nailed.

130

2) The bicycle-wheel spindle should be at least 6½ in long (or top bars LL sunk into back uprights BB, for example). The ball bearings are removed and the cones replaced so that they lock the spindle to the wheel-hub; it is best to put a rivet through the spindle (easy to drill), on the outside of one cone, to stop slipping. The spindle thread is filed away at the new bearing points (i.e. where it sits on the top bars). The round-bottomed notches in L should be the diameter of the newly-filed bearing points (still round, of course). There is a stiff leather collar (V) on the inner side of the front top bar (L) to stop the spindle from rising up on the downstroke of the treadle; this collar is fitted loosely on the spindle before the wheel-spindle assembly is dropped in place in the notches, then screwed or bolted into position.

3) The crank plate (W) is locked to the spindle end (pro-truding beyond back L) by a nut (bicycle original) on

32 Jura wheel, wheel hub-crank assembly

each side (Y is the inner nut). The crank plate is similarly locked to the crank bolt (X). The locking nuts, washers etc must be gauged to avoid friction between the crank-bolt locking nut on the inside of the crank plate (nut not visible in fig.33b) against the top bar (L) and, also, between the outer spindle-locking nut and the treadle rod; the latter can be planed down towards the end (fig.33b) to allow reduction of the length of the crank bolt, in turn reducing on the treadle's unwanted levering action on the wheel-spindle.

4) The circumference of the wheel will need partial filling and levelling, to give a regular driving-band surface and to increase momentum. Fill with heavy cord, anchored through the old valve hole to a spoke: wind round, tightly, until surface is level (crossways) but good rim still left on each side. Cord-end should be blended in smoothly. Then make a rubber band rather smaller (when relaxed) than the circumference of the wheel; this is easily done from the original bicycle inner-tube and rubber solution (edges just meeting on outside, joining patch on inside, for surface smoothness). Slip this band over the cord-filled rim. It should not be so wide that it runs up the inside walls of the rims since this would help the driving band to ride up and over the edge.

5) Tube (N) diameter can be varied to need, with S1 diameter adjusted to fit it. The collar (O) sits in a filed groove around the tube. The tube should be screwed on so that, when the flyer arms make a horizontal plane, the tube's elliptical outlet hole (made with a round-backed file) lies an eighth turn to the left of the tube's highest point (ie the hole leads straight to the nearest flyer hook — as wool direction in fig.31). The tube revolves in a $^7/8$ in hole in the front bar (F).

6) PQRS are best made from hardwoods.

7) P is cut out of planking (oak in fig.31). Its square-section hole fits the corresponding part of the spindle (S2), with two screws for extra rigidity. The hooks should be large, rounded, open, smooth; three or four are enough, on one arm only.

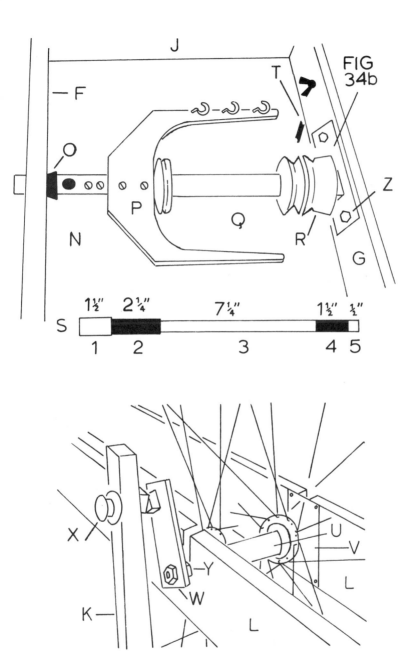

*33. Jura wheel. Upper: flyer-bobbin assembly, diagram (a)
Lower: hub-crank assembly, diagram (b)*

133

8) Q is lathe-turned, most easily in one piece but it could be made in three and glued together. The inner face of the flyer should be cut straight as should the ends of the bobbin (as right end in figs., not as traditionally-rounded left end — this was an experimental bobbin). The bobbin is drilled right through with a $5/8$ in round hole — the spindle within is ½ in diameter, round (S3).

9) R is also lathe-turned (ash). It has a square-section $3/8$ in hole corresponding to the spindle section (S4). Its smaller, squared extension has a hole to take a fine nut and bolt which run through a hole in the spindle, again for extra rigidity (both this and the screws in the flyer are optional).

10) The spindle (S) is made from a 13 x ¾" hard dowel rod, re-shaped over sections 2—5. The writer turns his own (ash), squaring off sections 2 and 4 with a rasp. Section 5 revolves in a ½ in hole in the back bar (G) or in the tensioning bar (see 12, below).

11) Friction can be reduced if both wheel and flyer-bobbin spindles revolve in holes in leather mounts, fixed to FG and back L (ie similar to the essential mount on the inside of front L), and not touching the wood. All turning points should be kept well oiled.

12) Tensioning device mounted *on* back bar (figs.33a, 34b, seen from front and back): spindle end (S5) revolves in hole in small bar held by two wing-nut bolts (1½-2 in, ZZ) in 2 in vertical slots in the back bar (G). To adjust tension, move the small bar up and down, clamping with the bolts.

13) Tensioning device *using* back bar (figs. 30, 34a): the back bar itself moves up and down on two 5—6 in wing-nut bolts (Z) running through the back uprights (BB). The back bar (G) again has 2 in vertical slots the width of the bolts.

14) Treadle-return rubber strips (figs. 31, 33a, 34: T) are simply fed through holes and knotted on further sides.

15) The hooks on the top of each back upright (BB) are for the skeins of yarn . . .

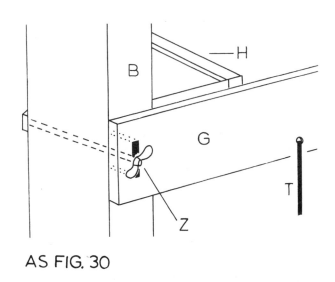

AS FIG. 30

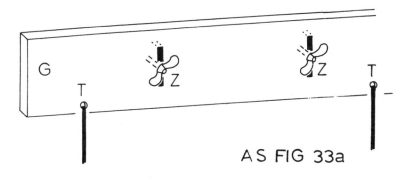

AS FIG 33a

34 Jura wheel, alternative tensioning devices (upper:a, lower:b)

35 The author's workshop, Jura

Further developments

A travelling bobbin or flyer has yet to be incorporated in the spinning wheel. A device for faster plying could be added, since this work is not linked to the spinner's teasing rate; in the meantime, the easiest way to achieve this is simply to have a 'plying wheel', a second wheel with both bobbin and flyer cogs smaller and, thus, a faster plying rate. Improved bearings are possible, of course: for example, the wheel-spindle could turn in a second bicycle-wheel's hubs, these cut away from the intervening axle and the spokes removed — the two hubs would be fixed in place of the leather mounts. The author would welcome discussion.

APPENDIX 1

SPINNING AND THERAPY

The spinning wheel's possibilities, as Gandhi saw, are not limited to the production of yarn. The rhythmic motion, the manipulative skill, the sight of the fibres flowing onto the bobbin — having a moment before been an unruly piece of fleece or bundle of flax fibres — these are relaxing, satisfying sensations. After perhaps a meaningless disordered day, even a short spinning session quietens and focusses the mind, so that the spinner rises in a calmer mood.

It is strange that the occupational therapy profession seems to have always preferred the complex craft of weaving for its patients — a craft many would-be weavers rapidly abandon as difficult and frustrating. Spinning is easier, it exercises the hands and legs gently and effortlessly, but persistently, whilst its rhythm and flow absorb a distracted mind.

It is common sense, too, that disturbed industrial man, his mind 'thwarted and distorted by the mechanisation of all that was once enjoyably primitive', in the words of the Commune Movement, should voluntarily regress himself to the moment of trauma in his technological childhood, so that he may understand his need for a craft or similar work. This holds good as much for the normal person in industrial society as for one in extreme need of therapy.

APPENDIX 2

SPINNING AND THE THIRD WORLD

As the distribution maps show (figs. 4, 5), many of the world's 'unadvanced' peoples do not spin or do so on a simple spindle or, in the case of the east, use a hand-turned rather than a treadled wheel. Present western practice is to 'aid' some of these societies. One opinion, however, considers this aid to be interference, although such peoples have usually already suffered interference in the form of varieties of exploitative development by western industry. Aid is currently divided, by those who favour it, into immediate relief and long-term self-development projects. Amongst the second are those designed and distributed by the 'appropriate technology' movement.

The introduction or technical advancing of a craft, such as spinning, seems worth considering where a people lacks the 'essentials' of life (the definition of which would vary from group to group and is happily outside the scope of this book). Many factors have to be considered. The availability of raw material, for example, and the effect of the new or increased demand on its producers. Possibly raw materials at present sent away unprocessed could be spun locally — as Gandhi saw for India — and perhaps dyed and woven locally too. However, it would have to be ensured that there were no vulnerable groups elsewhere who would be affected by not receiving these raw materials, or by other consequent changes.

The immediate social effects of the production of this new or increased yarn, whether used or sold, have to be considered. It might be that, if the current output can be produced faster, the spinners will be released for other useful work. But simply getting through the work more quickly may not be of value — the work may be enjoyed for its own sake or have a social function. The new ground-nut decorticators in a West African enterprise were deliberately kept to the simplest to avoid putting the wives out of work, with social consequences. Work, in the Buddhist sense of right livelihood, is a human need. There seems no justification for causing change if the people already have the essentials of food, clothing and housing.

The ITDG, already referred to in the first chapter, did feel, at its 1968 Conference, that 'in many cases modernisation of traditional methods is preferable to the revolutionary introduction of sophisticated machinery'. The craft of spinning generally meets Schumacher's 'appropriateness' criteria: labour intensiveness, the provision of work geographically within the community, a low-cost workshop, an easily-taught skill, the use of local raw materials, production for the community and not for export to and thus dependence on the rich countries.

Schumacher has also said of 'developing countries' that 'if the non-modern sector is not made the object of special development efforts, it will continue to disintegrate; this disintegration will continue to manifest itself in mass unemployment and mass migration into metropolitan areas . . .' Once this point is reached, it will be the first chapter which is more 'appropriate' to the society in question.

APPENDIX 3

SPINNING AND ECOLOGY

The effect of modern industry on the earth and its atmosphere does not need description. The spinning wheel belongs to the class of free, treadle-pedal machines which employ the energy of the human body, an energy this anyway needs to put out. The wheel's manufacture, suitable for the small-scale workshop, need use up neither raw materials nor industrial energy, as has been seen. The work itself, at least as envisaged in the opening pages, does not transgress the principles of the ecology movement. For example, during the 1970 Conservation Year, the International Youth Forum urged 'European Governments to adopt measures aimed at stabilisation of living standards and a limitation of blind economic growth, such as:

a) the cessation of continual and often trivial changes in fashion which affect the production of consumer goods . . .

c) production of quality durable goods to prevent continual wastage of natural resources.'

Collecting bottle-tops was not enough. In the US, a group called Ecology Action emphasizes individual action and personal ethics, aims at new life styles, rejects overproduction, lives economically and proposes reliance on oneself and one's friends rather than upon the industrial system.

APPENDIX 4

WOOL—MARKETING ORGANISATIONS

Australian Wool Corporation, Wool House, 578 Bourke St., Melbourne, 3000
International Wool Secretariat, 6—7 Carlton Gardens, London S.W.1
National Wool Growers Association, 600 Crandall Building, Salt Lake City, Utah; Suite 336, Southern Building, 805 — 15th St NW, Washington DC 20005
National Wool Marketing Corporation, 10 High Street, Boston, 10, Mass.
New Zealand Wool Marketing Corporation, 18 Brandon St., (PO Box 3849), Wellington CI
Wool Bureau of Canada Ltd., 2200 Yonge St., Toronto, Ontario.

British Wool Marketing Organisations

The British Wool Marketing Board itself is at Kew Bridge House, Kew Bridge Road, Brentford, Middlesex.
Its depots are:

South-West England

Devon & Cornwall Wools Ltd at Lamellion, Liskeard, Cornwall; Scarne Industrial Estate, Launceston, Cornwall; North Tawton, Devon; Chapel St., Buckfastleith, Devon; Pathfields, South Molton, Devon.

141

Southern England

Gregory, Prentis and Green Ltd., Mace Lane, Ashford, Kent; Kent Wool Growers Ltd., Brundrett House, Tannery Lane, Ashford, Kent; H & C Pearce & Sons Ltd., Lashlake, Thame, Oxon.

Central England

Scottish, English & Welsh Wool Growers Ltd., Lyonshall, Kington, Herefordshire
Francis Willey (H & C Pearce & Sons Ltd) at Farndon Rd, Market Harborough, Leics; Three Mills, Bromyard, Herefordshire.

Wales

Wool Producers of Wales Ltd at Dinas Mawddwy, Machynlleth, Powys; The Tannery, Brecon, Powys; Grove Rd, Denbigh, Clwyd; Cymric Mill, Newtown, Powys. TJ Williams (Tremadoc) Ltd at Garsiwn Lane, Machynlleth, Powys; Madoc St, Portmadoc, Gwynedd.

Northern England

North of England Wools Ltd. at Haugh Lane Industrial Estate, Hexham, Northumberland; Oak Mills, Station Road, Clayton, Bradford, W Yorks; Central Wool Growers Ltd., Priory Depot, Uffington Rd, Stamford, Lincs; Scottish, English & Welsh Wool Growers Ltd, Watson Wool Depot, Carnforth, Lancs.
Norman Trees Ltd, 23 Wellington St., Ripon, N. Yorks.
Wool Warehouses Ltd., Threeply Mills, 99 East Parade, Bradford, W. Yorks.
Yorkshire & Northern Wool Growers Ltd., 12 Park Rd., Norton, Malton, N. Yorks.

Scotland

Caledonian Wools Ltd at:
   John Dun & Co Ltd, Valley Mills, Galashiels, Selkirkshire.

J & W Greig (Wools) Ltd, Dalmonach Works, Bonhill, Alexandria, Dunbartonshire
Mactaggart Bros (Fleece) Ltd, Burnsfoot Industrial Estate, Hawick, Roxburghshire
Stewart & Ramsden Ltd at Mitchelston Drive, Mitchelston Industrial Estate, Kirkcaldy, Fife; North Wheatlands Mill, Galashiels, Selkirkshire.
William C Scott Ltd, 72 East Dock Street, Dundee.
Scottish, English & Welsh Wool Growers Ltd at Nithsdale Mill, St Michael St., Dumfries; P. O. Box 25, Underwood Wool Stores, Brown Street, Paisley, Renfrewshire; Newton Road, Evanton, Ross-shire.

Northern Ireland

Ulster Wools Ltd, 20 Tirgracey Rd, Muackamore, Co. Antrim.

The rest of Britain's two hundred merchants will be found listed in *Skinner's British Textile Register,* a year-book published from RAC House, Lansdowne Road, Croydon.

APPENDIX 5

SOCIETIES, MUSEUMS AND OTHER BODIES

Communes Network, c/o Laurieston Hall, Castle Douglas, Kirkcudbrightshire

Botanical gardens (fibre plants)

Festival Spinning Workshop, Edinburgh, teaches throughout each festival, late August to mid-September (run by the author at 21 Barony Street, Edinburgh 3)

Guilds of spinners in Britain, see *Quarterly Journal* of the Dyers, Spinners and Weavers Guilds.

Historisk Arkaeologisk Forsøgcenter, 4230 Lejre, Denmark — specialised in primitive textiles

Intermediate Technology Development Group, Parnell House, 25 Wilton Road, London SW1

Museums (UK) specialising in spinning tools: Bath (American), Belfast, Glasgow, Halifax (Bankfield), London (Science), Manchester.

Rare Breeds Survival Trust, Cotswold Farm Park, Guiting Power, Cheltenham, Gloucester.

Suppliers of materials, tools etc: see Allen J, *Guide to Craft Suppliers* (Studio Vista, London 1974)

Zoos (raw materials visible and, sometimes, available)

BIBLIOGRAPHY

Ågren, K, *Västerbottenisk textiltradition* (Sweden, Umeå 1974)

Allaby, M, *The Eco-Activists* (London 1971)

Anon., *The Book of English Trades* (1824)

Bell, HS, *Wool* (London 1970)

British Wool Marketing Board, *British Sheep Breeds* (London 1967)

British Wool Marketing Board, *Growing Wool* (Wakefield 1972)

Burnley, J, *The History of Wool and Woolcombing* (London 1889)

Chadwick, J, 'Alternative Culture', *Marxism Today* (London, March 1976)

Commune Movement, *Manifesto: A Federal Society based on the Free Commune* (no date)

Diderot, D, *Encyclopédie* (France c.1750)

Dobson, BP, *The Evolution of the Spinning Machine* (c.1911)

Ellacot, SE, *Spinning and Weaving* (London, 1956)

Endrei, W, *L'Evolution des Techniques du Filage et du Tissage* (Paris 1968)

Forbes, RJ, *Studies in Technology,* Vol. IV (Leiden 1956)

Forde, CD, *Habitat, Economy and Society* (London 1934)

Gilbert, KR, *Textile Machinery* (HMSO 1971)

Grant, IF, *Highland Folkways* (London 1961)

Haughton, R, 'Communities: Example and Symbol', *Community* 14 (Spring 1976)

Henderson, P, *William Morris, his life, work and friends* (London 1967)

Henshall, AS, 'Textile & Weaving Appliances in Pre-historic Britain', *Proceedings of the Prehistoric Society* N.S.16 (1950)

Hoffman, M, 'The Great wheel in Scandinavian Countries', *Studies in Folk Life,* ed. Jenkins, JG (London 1969)

Huxley, A, *After Many a Summer* (London 1939)

ITDG, *Conference Report: The Further Development in the UK of Appropriate Technologies and their communication to Developing Countries* (London 1968)

Jenkins, JG, *The Welsh Woollen Trade* (Cardiff 1969)

Jenkins, JG, ed, *The Wool Textile Industry in Great Britain* (London 1972)

Lattimore, O, *Mongol Journeys* (London 1941)

Lipson, E, *The Woollen and Worsted Industries* (London 1921)

Lipson, E, *The Economic History of England* (London 1961)

Macdonald, DK, *Fibres, Spindles and Spinning Wheels* (Ontario 1950)

Mercer, J, *Canary Islands: Fuerteventura* (Newton Abbot 1973)

Mercer, J, *Hebridean Islands: Colonsay, Gigha, Jura* (Glasgow 1974)

Mercer, J, *Spanish Sahara* (London 1976)

Morris, W, *Collected Works,* ed Morris, M (London 1910–15)

Morton, WE & Wray, GR, *An Introduction to the Study of Spinning* (London 1962)

Napier, J, *Manufacturing Arts of Ancient Times* (London 1874)

Onions, WJ, *Wool* (London 1962)

Ross, A, *Scottish Home Industries* (Dingwall 1895)

Ryder, ML, 'The History of Sheep in Scotland', *Bradford Textile Society* (1967–8)

Ryder, ML, & Stephenson, SK, *Wool Growth* (London & New York, 1968)

Ryder, ML, *Animal Bones in Archaeology* (Mammal Society of the British Isles: 1969)

Schumacher, EF, *Small is Beautiful* (London 1973)

Singer, C, *A History of Technology* (London 1954–8)

Spinners, Dyers and Weavers Guild, *Quarterly Journal*

Thompson, F, *Harris Tweed* (Newton Abbot 1969)

Thompson, GB, *Spinning Wheels* (Belfast 1964)

Weir, S, *Spinning and Weaving in Palestine* (British Museum 1970)

Wool Intelligence, monthly journal

Yates, J, *The Art of Spinning among the Ancients* (London 1843)

INDEX

148